TO: _____

FROM: _____

DATE: _____

# Jesus, I Need You

## HONEST PRAYERS FROM A TRUSTING HEART

**ZONDERVAN®**

ZONDERVAN

*Jesus, I Need You*
Copyright © 2015, 2017 by Zondervan

Requests for information should be addressed to:
Zondervan, *3900 Sparks Dr. SE, Grand Rapids, Michigan 49546*

ISBN 978-0-3100-8829-5

# Contents

# Jesus, I Need Your . . . Guidance

# I Need You

Dear Jesus,

Sometimes it's so easy for me to forget just how much I need You. How many times have You tried to tell me something, and I haven't listened? I *need* to listen more to Your soft, quiet voice. And how often have You tried to show me something, but I haven't seen? I *need* to open my eyes to Your presence all around me. I *need* to take time to look up at the sky and down at the earth and to recognize the amazing works of Your hands. I *need* to open my heart to the needs of others so I can sympathize and empathize with them and serve them better.

Dear Jesus, I need *You*. With every day, every minute, every breath, I need You. Teach me to seek You more each day. Remind me that unless I take time to draw near to You, I will struggle to hear Your voice and to see all You have to show me. Jesus, when I read my Bible, reveal Yourself to me through Your words. Fill my heart with Your love and my spirit with Your strength. Wipe away the world's distractions, and help me focus on You.

I need You, Jesus.

*And my God will meet all your needs according to the riches of his glory in Christ Jesus.*

—PHILIPPIANS 4:19

We all *need* Jesus. Not only does He save us from our sins and open the way to heaven for us, Jesus also longs to save us from anything that stands in the way of our relationships with Him. Is there something keeping you from drawing nearer to Jesus? Write a prayer asking Jesus to remove anything that stands between you and Him. Ask Him to help you draw ever closer to Him.

Dear Jesus, please remove any distractions that keep me from spending time w/ you. Also, remove the laziness that's in me and help me to not become so angry so quickly. Give me patience restore my heart and Spirit for I long to be w/ you. I love you and miss you and really need you back in my life.

In the name of Jesus, Amen.

# Scattered Thoughts

Dear Jesus,

My thoughts are so scattered today. The anxiety that comes with too many things to do and trying to get them all done makes my chest tighten and my mind spin out of control. I'm having trouble capturing my thoughts and organizing them so that I can come up with a clear and productive plan.

Lord, the what-ifs and if-onlys keep sneaking into my head and stealing my ability to concentrate on what I need to do. They whisper and taunt me: *What if I can't do this? What if I can't get it done in time? If only I didn't have so much to do! If only I had someone to help me!* Oh, Lord, help me remember that I do have Someone to help me—I have You!

Why is it so hard for me to remember to call on You first? I know You're always with me and ready to help. I ask You to help me now, Lord Jesus. Remove all these what-ifs and if-onlys from my mind. Show me what is truly important. Sweep away what's unnecessary and unproductive. Jesus, You are my strength and my help. Together, we will do what needs to be done.

*We demolish arguments and every pretension that sets itself up against the knowledge of God, and we take captive every thought to make it obedient to Christ.*

*—2 CORINTHIANS 10:5*

What-ifs and if-onlys can scatter your thoughts, leaving you anxious and tangled up in knots. That's when you need to lean on Jesus. Let Him be the calm in your storm. Take a moment to write down all those things you believe you need to do. Pray over your list, and ask Jesus to sift through it—to reveal what most needs your attention, what can wait, and what isn't yours to do.

- Renewal of (Spirit) ♥
- Studying and taking the ATI PEAS TEST (Passing)
- Achieving good grades ✓
- Deciding what to do with my relationship.
- praying always (Starting in the Mornings)
- Setting time aside for Worshiping Jesus.

Setting free by giving all my burdens to the Lord, God, and

Savior Jesus, Amen

# Learning to Trust

Dear Jesus,

I have a confession to make: I'm afraid of entrusting everything to You. In my head, I know that You love me and want only the best for me. But in my heart, it's still so hard to give up every aspect of my life to Your care. When I have trouble, I'm eager to give You my problems. But when things are going well—the way *I* think they should—I'm not so eager to give up control. I'm not so eager to give You my everything.

Jesus, I struggle with not knowing. If I give You everything, what will You do with it? Will You make big changes? Will You take me places I'm not sure I want to go? Will there be valleys along the way or mountains to climb?

I should just trust You. And I do *want* to trust You. So why is this so hard for me? You know me perfectly, Lord, inside and out. So I pray that You will help me conquer this struggle. Teach me that I don't need to be afraid. Help me give You everything. Please take my hand and lead me gently, one step at a time, ever closer to You.

> "For I know the plans I have for you," declares the
> Lord, "plans to prosper you and not to harm you,
> plans to give you hope and a future."
>
> —JEREMIAH 29:11

Handing over everything to God isn't easy. It requires trust, and that can be especially difficult if anyone has ever betrayed your trust. But remember that God is perfect—perfectly faithful and perfectly worthy of your trust. He will never betray you or let you down. Think of a time when you experienced God's faithfulness—in your own life or in the life of someone you know. How can that experience help you trust God with everything today?

Trusting has become a bit hard lately. Extermely, hard actually. Ryan and I betrayed each other and ever since then it's gone downhill. Sometimes, I feel like I can't even trust my mom. And in a way She's the only person I can really depend on. But I don't even have her, at times.

Psalms 27:10
Reminds me that if I lost everything and only had you, you'd be my everything.

# When I Am Tempted

Dear Jesus,

Why is self-control so difficult? Whether it's overeating, spending too much time on my phone, or losing my temper, sometimes my self-control slips, and I do the very thing that I don't want to do.

How I wish I didn't have to struggle with right and wrong! But I do know that I never have to struggle alone. Jesus, You've promised to help me stand strong against temptation. I must remember to call upon You and Your strength when my self-control is put to the test. But even before temptation comes, I need to be ready—just as You were ready when Satan tempted You. Help me arm myself with Scripture, just as You did, so I can fight off the enemy's attacks. Fill me with Your kind of strength, the kind that comes from trusting the Father.

Jesus, I know You are always with me, and I'm so thankful. You fill in the gaps left by my imperfections. I trust You, Jesus, to keep me safe and to make me strong.

*Because he himself suffered when he was tempted,*
*he is able to help those who are being tempted.*

—HEBREWS 2:18

*- preparation*
*- calling upon God*

Temptation is all around us, but Jesus taught us how to overcome it. Read Matthew 4:1–11. When temptation came, Jesus was <u>prepared</u> by being armed with the Word of God. What are your temptations? Spend some time in God's Word, searching for verses that will arm you against those temptations. Then record them here as a ready reference for when trouble comes.

_____

_____

_____

_____

_____

_____

_____

_____

_____

_____

_____

_____

_____

_____

_____

_____

_____

_____

_____

# In Prayer

Dear Jesus,

Today I realized that I've been giving You instructions when I pray. You already know all that I want, and You also know what I truly need. But when I've prayed, I've told You exactly how I think You should answer my prayer. I've laid my plans before You and asked You to bless them—instead of seeking Your plans for me. Prayer doesn't work that way, and I'm sorry.

Jesus, I am so used to being in control. I'm supposed to control the things in my home, in my activities, and in so many areas of my life. It's my responsibility to make sure that everything runs smoothly. But it's not my responsibility to control You or the plans You have for me.

Your answers to my prayers are so much better than mine; I believe that, Lord. You know exactly whether to say yes, no, or not right now. And when You say no, I can be certain that Your plan is a better one. I trust You and Your goodness.

I want to pray that Your will be done in all things, Jesus, but sometimes I get ahead of myself. Sometimes I forget to let You take control. Forgive me.

*Many are the plans in a person's heart,*
*but it is the LORD's purpose that prevails.*
*—PROVERBS 19:21*

If anyone knew about prayer, it was Corrie ten Boom, the Dutch woman who was imprisoned for helping Jews escape the Nazis during WWII. About prayer, she said, "It is not our task to give God instructions. We are simply to report for duty."[1] Prayer isn't only about making your needs known to the Lord, but it's also about trusting the perfection and goodness of His answer. Today, write a prayer of surrender, telling God you trust Him to take control.

# My Helper

Dear Jesus,

I'm not very good at some things—You and I both know what those things are. Whether it's the things in my day-to-day life or it's my spiritual stubbornness, I find myself wrestling with the same struggles over and over again. Jesus, I'm trying. And with Your help and Your strength, I'll keep trying. I know You'll help me overcome these struggles, and I'll slowly get better at the things I find so difficult to do.

I'm learning to breathe, relax, and turn my thoughts over to You. You help me think more clearly. You've taught me to tackle these difficult things in prayer first and then to take them one step at a time, with You by my side. I trust You to help me along the way, and You give me hope that I can accomplish what I need to do—and, more important, what You want me to do. When I surrender myself and let You lead me through a difficult task, then I am confident—because there is nothing that You and I can't do together!

So thank You, Jesus. Thank You for always being my help and my hope.

*I lift up my eyes to the mountains—*
*where does my help come from?*
*My help comes from the LORD.*

*—PSALM 121:1-2*

When you face a difficult task, call on Jesus for help. His wisdom will guide you. Ask Him to lead your thoughts and help you focus on what you need to get done, what He wants you to do. Read Proverbs 3:5. When you face a challenge, do you lean on your own understanding? How could you demonstrate your trust in the Lord and lean on Jesus instead?

# I Surrender All

Dear Jesus,

How many times have I laid everything at Your feet: my problems, my hopes, my prayers, my life? I've surrendered it all to You . . . only to snatch it all right back again. I've worried over problems and tried to fix things myself instead of entrusting them to Your perfect care.

Lord, I *do* trust You. I *am* willing to hand over my everything to You. And I *do* believe that You work everything both for my good and Your glory. But, Lord, I need Your help to live out what I believe. Teach me to wait patiently and expectantly for Your solutions to my problems and Your answers to my prayers. And when I'm impatient and snatch back my troubles so that I can worry over them some more, please forgive me. Remind me yet again that You've got everything under control.

Once more, Lord, I surrender everything to You—and I don't want it back. Help me leave it all with You.

*"Blessed is the one who trusts in the LORD,*
*whose confidence is in him.*
*They will be like a tree planted by the water*
*that sends out its roots by the stream."*
—JEREMIAH 17:7-8

"All to Jesus, I surrender; all to Him I freely give; I will ever love and trust Him, in His presence daily live"—so begins the classic hymn written by Judson Van DeVenter. More than a hundred years old, these beloved words still echo with the struggle to surrender everything to Jesus.[1] As you read the words of this hymn, what comes to mind that you need to surrender to Jesus? How can you better live "in His presence" this day?

# Guide Me, Please Guide Me

Dear Jesus,

From the day I first chose to follow You, I've prayed that I would grow stronger in my faith. I've prayed that I would draw just a little closer to You as I follow You all the days of my life.

Some days it's easy. I read Your Word, and I praise You in song. Faith is effortless, and trusting You is a joy. But others days, it's not so easy. I feel attacked, as if the world is conspiring to pull me away from You. Sometimes the attacks are sudden and intense. I recognize them, and they send me running straight to You for protection, for guidance. But more often, they creep in on me, slowly distracting me until I wake up with a start and realize I drifted too far away from You.

So I offer up this prayer. Shield me from attack, protect me from these insidious distractions. Every step, every word, every thought—I surrender to Your guidance. Shore up the wall of my faith so that the enemy cannot breach it.

Thank You, Jesus, for being my faithful and ever-present guide.

*Guide me in your truth and teach me,*
*for you are God my Savior,*
*and my hope is in you all day long.*
*—PSALM 25:5*

The attacks of the enemy, the evil one, are real. First Peter 5:8 warns, "Be alert and of sober mind. Your enemy the devil prowls around like a roaring lion looking for someone to devour." It can be a frightening thought, until you remember who your Savior is and the truth that He has already defeated the evil one (John 16:33). Psalm 25 is David's beautiful prayer for protection and guidance while under attack. Rewrite this prayer in your own words, applying it to the attacks you face in your own life.

# How Should I Decide?

Dear Jesus,

I have a decision to make, but I first want to thank You for blessing me so richly. You have set before me two attractive paths, and I'm grateful for the opportunities they offer. But Jesus, deciding which one to take is so hard. I've been praying—and I know You've been listening—but so far I haven't felt You guide me toward one way or the other. What should I do?

I've thought hard about it. I've listed all the advantages and disadvantages for each. But the truth is that both paths seem to be blessings—just very different blessings. And I'm not sure what to do. I want to do what's right and what pleases You, but I need Your help to figure that out.

Guide me with Your wisdom. I've searched Your Word, looking for direction, and I've prayed. Now I need You to speak to me. I know I can't stay stuck in this place of indecision, and my time to decide is running out. Tell me, dear Jesus. What path should I choose? I trust You to guide me.

*Blessed are those who find wisdom,*
*those who gain understanding....*
*Her ways are pleasant ways,*
*and all her paths are peace.*
—PROVERBS 3:13, 17

When faced with a tough decision, it's always important to pray for guidance and to search the Bible for answers. But sometimes—especially when both options are good—God leaves the decision up to you. Read Proverbs 3:6. How does this verse offer peace for the decisions you must make?

# Light My Way

Dear Jesus,

I feel like a ship lost at sea. My eyes, my soul search through the dark night, looking for a welcoming beacon on the shore, looking for You. Jesus, I need the light that is You. I need You to guide me home, to guide me back to You.

Your Word promises that if I search for You, then You will be found. So I am searching, Lord. Guide me through the pages of Your Word and enlighten me. Strengthen my faith and my trust in You.

My belief has been shaken, Lord, but I will not give up on You. I know that You have not left me—will never leave me—but I have drifted from You. The truth is that I am weak, and You are so strong and so wise that Your ways are beyond my understanding. Right now, all that is human in me feels raw and abandoned, though I know I am not.

Sweet Jesus, light my way back to You. Draw me close to Your side. Restore my relationship with You because You are what my heart and my soul need.

*Search me, God, and know my heart;*
*test me and know my anxious thoughts.*
*See if there is any offensive way in me,*
*and lead me in the way everlasting.*
—PSALM 139:23–24

Has some event left you questioning your faith? When a Christian feels far from Jesus, it is a lonely, frightening feeling. Pour out your fears and worries on this page. Be completely honest with yourself and with God. Then pray and dig deep into the Word. Answer each of your worries and fears with a promise from God.

# Reflections on Guidance

# Reflections on Guidance

# Jesus, I Need You . . . When I Feel Overwhelmed

# I Can't Do It Myself

Dear Jesus,

My faith tells me that You are with me. I really *do* believe that. But sometimes You seem so far away. I'm tired, weary, and overwhelmed by all that is expected of me. It seems as if everyone wants a piece of me, and I have nothing left to give. I'm trying to please everyone, encourage and support everyone, love everyone. I have poured out everything I have, and now I feel empty, frustrated, and alone.

There are days when I just want to shout at the people around me: "Don't you know that I need encouragement, support, and love too?" But I don't shout. I fake a smile and just keep going. I know You love me and will support me, so I try to lean on You. I trust that You are with me—but I need to *feel* Your presence with me, in my heart.

Jesus, I can't do it all by myself, and You tell me I'm not supposed to. The truth is that I'm having trouble holding it together, and I need You. Wrap me in Your love, and quiet this turmoil inside me. Fill me with Your comfort, strength, and peace. Jesus, take these overwhelming burdens from me and give me rest.

*"Come to me, all you who are weary and burdened, and I will give you rest."*

—MATTHEW 11:28

Attacking life with an "I can do it myself" attitude can end up draining you and pushing Jesus away. Why? Because you were created to depend on Him and not on yourself. Consider all the obligations you feel you must meet. Have you invited Jesus and His guidance into each of these situations? How might His presence help you find quiet time to rest and to be still with Him?

# We're in This Together

Dear Jesus,

I have so much to do—I'm not even sure where to start. I have errands to run, bills to pay, cards to write, and all the other endless tasks of everyday life. And then there are all the things I feel I should be doing for friends, for family, for You. But even though I'm busy all the time, I feel as if I'm spinning my wheels and getting nowhere. Just when I think I have things under control, something unexpected happens.

And then there's that word, Lord—*control*. When will I learn that I cannot control every aspect of my life? You remind me of that so often, and yet I try to do it anyway.

Jesus, I want You to be in control of my life *and* my to-do list. Shape my priorities. Show me what You want me to do. Remind me, please, that it's okay to say no sometimes, and please remove any distractions that get in my way. Give me a cheerful heart as I tackle those things that truly need to be done.

I feel better now, Lord, because I know that we're in this together.

"Obey everything I have commanded you. And surely I am with you always, to the very end of the age."

—MATTHEW 28:20

No matter how long your to-do list becomes, it's important to take time for Jesus each day. Allow Him to refresh and renew you, to guide you with His wisdom. Write out a commitment to spend time with Jesus each day. Include how you will spend that time with Him—in prayer, reading, or quiet thoughts of praise.

# I'm Worn-Out

Dear Jesus,

I feel completely overwhelmed. Every part of me is worn-out. I'm physically, mentally, and spiritually exhausted. My body aches from all the stress—it surrounds me and presses down on me until I can barely breathe. My mind overflows with worry. Scenes from past mistakes and heartaches play in my mind like old movies. And I wonder, *Was there more that I could have done? Did I do the right things? Did I make any difference at all?* Please come and quiet my soul, Lord Jesus.

You seem so far away, but Your Word promises that You are near. So I hold tight to my faith, I believe in the truth that You haven't abandoned me. And I *do* believe, Lord. You are a good and loving Shepherd, and I know that You will never leave this hurting lamb alone. I trust that You will somehow take all this chaos and make something wonderful from it.

Please, Lord Jesus, let me find rest under the shelter of Your wings.

*My soul is weary with sorrow;*
*strengthen me according to your word.*
*Keep me from deceitful ways;*
*be gracious to me and teach me your law.*
—PSALM 119:28-29

When your burdens become too heavy to carry, Jesus is there, ready to take them, ready to give your soul rest. When you are too weary to walk, He carries you in His arms. And when your prayers are reduced to "Help," "Please," and "Hurry," Jesus hears and pulls you even closer to His heart. Take a moment to pour out your thoughts, fears, and feelings to Him. Don't worry about getting the words just right; simply tell everything to Jesus. He listens, and He understands.

# A Weary Traveler

Dear Jesus,

What is this journey I am on? The road has been so long, and Jesus, You know the obstacles I've faced along the way. My path keeps twisting and turning. Sometimes it even doubles back and sends me in circles. How long, dear Jesus, before I reach my destination? What is that beautiful but secret goal You have planned for me?

Where are You leading me, Lord? Just when I think I know, You surprise me with a fork in the road. You send me in a new direction, one that I never expected. Sometimes I just want to stop for a while, but You know me so well. You know that if I were to stop now, I might never continue on.

All along the way, You have been with me. You've listened to my prayers. You've kept watch over me. You know what I want, and You know even better than I what I need. I trust You, Jesus, but are we almost there? I am weary and ready to rest, but still I will follow You.

*Commit your way to the LORD;*
*trust in him and he will do this:*
*he will make your righteous reward*
*shine like the dawn.*
*—PSALM 37:5-6*

Have you been traveling down a long road? Have there been unexpected events, unanticipated twists and turns? God knows where this road ends; trust Him, rest in Him, and allow Him to lead you. Think back over the journey of your life. How far have you come? In what ways have you seen God's faithfulness? Do those give you hope and reassurance for the road ahead?

# Moving Mountains

Dear Jesus,

When I look at everything I need to do, it's all too much for me. Often it's so much that I just sit and do nothing—I can't seem to get started because I don't know where to begin. Procrastination is such a problem for me, Lord, because while I'm overwhelmed and doing nothing, the pile of to-dos just grows bigger and bigger. Please help me.

I need strength to dig in and get going. I need You to help me focus on one task at a time and turn my eyes away from this mountain of stuff. I need strength to zero in on one task at a time and keep moving forward.

And Jesus, I need help with giving myself credit for the tasks that I *do* accomplish, instead of scolding myself because I didn't get everything done. Help me set smaller, more reasonable and realistic goals—goals I can actually achieve. Then celebrate with me when I achieve them.

I know that with Your strength and Your guidance, we can get this done. Please keep my eyes focused on You instead of on the mountain.

*The LORD makes firm the steps*
*of the one who delights in him.*
—PSALM 37:23

Has your mountain of "stuff" grown so big that it seems impossible to knock down? Think about Jesus and His ministry. He worked steadily, task by task, need by need, often helping just one person at a time. Follow Jesus' example. Start now and write down one thing you can get done today—just one. Ask Jesus to help you focus on accomplishing this one thing. How might tackling things one at a time help you "move your mountain"?

# Singing a New Song

Dear Jesus,

I find myself complaining so often. Sometimes I hear the words coming out of my mouth, and I just cringe. I complain whenever I have too much work to do. I complain about chores around the house. I complain that I don't have enough help, and I complain that there aren't enough hours in my day. I allow everyday tasks to weigh me down, and then I complain to whoever will listen—and most often I complain to You.

"Oh, Jesus," I say, "I'm too busy. I need more help. I need You to take this stress away from me. I need more time for me. I need the people in my life to be more understanding." And yes, there is some truth to all that, but what I really need is to change my attitude. When I praise You instead of complaining to You, I feel the burdens lift.

So help me, dear Jesus. Help me choose to see all that is good and pure, all that is wonderful and worthy of praise—instead of all that is worthy of complaint. Teach me to sing a new song.

*Sing to the LORD a new song;*
*sing to the LORD, all the earth.*
*Sing to the LORD, praise his name.*
*—PSALM 96:1-2*

Do you catch yourself complaining a lot? It's an easy habit to slip into, and it might be time for a change in attitude. Make a list of the things you complain about most often. Then, beside each complaint, note something about it that you can be thankful for, something you can praise God for. Make *this* your new habit: turning complaints into praise.

# Good News, Bad News

Dear Jesus,

I need some good news! It seems lately that every newscast begins with a story about some crime or terrible tragedy. The front page of the newspaper almost always features bad news. Disasters and sadness are everywhere, and it's overwhelming me. Where has all the good news gone?

This world is Yours, Lord. With so many good people following Your example and doing good things, there must be some positive things that are newsworthy. But if the world hears about them at all, they're usually tucked away at the end of the newscast or the last page of the paper, taking a backseat to evil.

Dear Jesus, I know in my heart that You can turn this around. Take the attention from this glut of bad news, and turn the world's eyes toward You. And turn my eyes toward You. Reveal to me Your goodness and Your beauty—I know they are everywhere, all around me.

> Finally, brothers and sisters, whatever is true, whatever is noble, whatever is right, whatever is pure, whatever is lovely, whatever is admirable—if anything is excellent or praiseworthy—think about such things.
>
> —PHILIPPIANS 4:8

It does seem that bad news so often outweighs good news. But don't allow that to overwhelm you. Dig a little deeper for the good news, and choose to dwell on that instead of the bad. Read Philippians 4:8. How many good and pure and lovely things can you see today? Write out a praise to Jesus, thanking Him for each and every one.

# The Rush and Hurry

Dear Jesus,

It's been such a long day. I started the day in a hurried rush, and it hasn't slowed down since. I rush at home, I rush around town, and then I rush home to hurry some more. How did my life get so busy?

I find myself daydreaming of quiet things—a cup of coffee while lingering over the newspaper, a hot bath while reading a novel, even simply sitting and gazing out the window. But moments of stillness are so elusive. I need them, though, Lord. I need peace. In truth, Lord, I need You.

Open up my days. Create in them moments to slip away, to hide away with You. And help me to take advantage of them. Refresh me, renew me, shower me with Your calming peace. Teach me to take deep, quiet breaths—even in the midst of the chaos—*especially* in the midst of the chaos.

And when the world gets too frantic for me, I will choose to rush and to hurry . . . right to You.

*"But seek first his kingdom and his righteousness, and all these things will be given to you as well."*

—MATTHEW 6:33

This world is in such a hurry—and if you're not careful, it will drag you along into its frenzy. The danger of rushing is that it keeps you distracted. It keeps you thinking about anything and everything except the quiet strength of Christ. Determine to be different. Take ten minutes—just ten minutes—and spend them simply sitting quietly, thinking about the presence of God with you. At the end of those minutes, note how you feel.

# I Can Choose

Dear Jesus,

You've taught me something. When I feel pressed down by some situation, I can *choose*—and with Your help, I have the ability—to turn things around.

When I am weighed down by negative comments, I can respond positively. I can *choose* to answer, "It's so hot and humid out today" with a more joyful, "Yes, but look at that beautiful blue sky!" If my to-do list is too long, I don't have to be afraid to admit it. I can *choose* to ask for help. And if someone wants me to do "just one little thing" when I already have too much to do, I can *choose* to say no.

Why did it take me so long to learn this? *You* are my example, Jesus. Even though You could do anything, You didn't try to do everything all by Yourself. You chose to have helpers. Your choices turn the negative into something positive. When I put my faith in You and allow You to direct my steps, then I can choose to do that too.

Help me, Lord, to choose the joyful instead the bleak, to choose the encouraging rather than the discouraging. Help me, Lord, to choose You.

*I have considered my ways*
*and have turned my steps to your statutes.*
—PSALM 119:59

When you feel overwhelmed by negativity or simply have too much to do, remember that you can choose to turn it around! The first thing Jesus did in His ministry was to enlist disciples to help Him. What are some things you need help with? And whom can you ask to help you? Are there other negatives in your life that you can turn into positives by the choices you make?

# Overwhelmed with Joy

Dear Jesus,

The word *overwhelmed* means to be flooded with too much of something. Usually, being overwhelmed is seen as something negative. Usually, but not always—because, Lord, how wonderful it is to be overwhelmed by You!

Every day You bless me in so many little ways—too many to count. Then, when those big blessings come along, I am completely overwhelmed. You bless me beyond anything I could ever ask or imagine—with unconditional love, unearned grace, endless mercy, and the promise of heaven with You. I am humbled by the height and width and depth of Your love and care for me.

With unending strength and power, You protect me from evil. Your presence surrounds, comforts, and shields me when life presses down hard. I am awed by Your constant faithfulness and gentleness, by Your ability to bring goodness from all things.

When I think of how You chose to suffer and die for my sins, I am overcome by both sadness and joy. You sacrificed Yourself so that I might live with You forever. What an amazing gift!

I am overwhelmed by the joy of You, Jesus.

*Because he was full of grace and truth, we*
*all received one gift after another.*

—JOHN 1:16 NCV

Just knowing Jesus and experiencing His mercy, grace, and love are overwhelming gifts. Think of all the blessings He showers on you each day: little blessings, like the sweet song of a sparrow outside your window, and big blessings, like resolving difficult problems or mending a broken relationship. There's an old hymn that challenges you to "count your many blessings." Accept that challenge today, and name your blessings "one by one."

# Reflections on Feeling Overwhelmed

# Reflections on Feeling Overwhelmed

Jesus, I Need You . . . When I Feel Gratitude

# Bring Out the Best

Dear Jesus,

You bring out the best in me. When I am compassionate, kind, caring, or selfless, it is because I have followed Your example. When I work to serve others, it is really You working through me. You create in me a desire to work harder and better because I want others to see You in me.

And Jesus, You give the best to me. Every day You open my eyes to so many little things that fill my heart with joy: a child's laughter, a friendly smile, the sunrise, the soft sound of gentle rain. You give me strength when I'm weak and courage when I'm frightened. Because You calm my storms, I am able to comfort others. You forgive me, and by Your example, I am able to forgive others. You are always good and right, so I can always trust You to help me make good and right choices in my life.

Whatever happens, I know You are with me. You are my Savior, my guide, and my very best friend. I love You, Jesus. Thank You for bringing out the best in me.

*Even more, I consider everything to be nothing compared to knowing Christ Jesus my Lord. To know him is worth much more than anything else.*

—PHILIPPIANS 3:8 NIRV

Jesus brings out the best in you when you put Him first in your life. As you try to follow His example and be more like Him, you'll feel His presence growing in your life. Is there an aspect of your life in which you need to be more like Jesus? What is something you can do today to better reflect Him and His love to the world around you?

# What a Beautiful Day!

Dear Jesus,

Today is a lovely day because You love me. And I see that love all around me in this world You created. Yes, the perfection of the Garden of Eden is gone, stolen by sin. But even in this fallen world, I see the work of Your hands. Only You could bless the bird with its song or tell the wind what to whisper through the trees. Only You could paint such sunsets or send the sunrise bursting across the skies. Only You could build up mountains, carve out oceans, and send the meadows skipping across the plains. And only You, Lord, could create me.

Jesus, if *this* world—with all its fallen imperfections—holds so much beauty and wonder, I can only imagine the beauty and wonder to be found in the perfection of heaven. And it's because of Your great love, Your gift of grace, that heaven is waiting for me—with a sky more perfect than this sky, a warmth more welcoming than the sun, and sounds sweeter than any bird's song.

Oh, Jesus, thank You for this lovely day! I am so blessed.

> "See, I am doing a new thing!
> Now it springs up; do you not perceive it?
> I am making a way in the wilderness
> and streams in the wasteland."
> —ISAIAH 43:19

The artist Minnie Aumonier wrote, "There is always music amongst the trees in the garden, but our hearts must be very quiet to hear it." God's amazing creation is all around you. Do you see it? Do you hear it? Only God could create that! Take a moment to quiet your heart and soak up the beauty that surrounds you. Then write out a prayer of praise for God's perfection in this imperfect world.

# Thank You for Joy

Dear Jesus,

Sometimes I crave the unbridled joy of childhood. I remember how it felt to pedal my bike fast, wind whipping through my hair, without a care in the world. I long for the innocence of seeing life through a child's eyes, to laugh, sing, and play again.

With each passing year, I feel as if my joy has been pushed deeper down inside me. But Jesus, You show me that true joy is found in more than just worldly happiness. Joy is in the reassurance of Your presence, the contentment of knowing Your love. It is in Your creation, in the beauty of the earth. It is in a smile, a kind word, a laugh, and a song. But most of all, joy is found in worship and praise and in thankfulness for You.

Yes, worldly happiness is temporary, but Your joy is eternal. It exists no matter what my circumstances may be. It is finding joyful innocence in my grown-up heart. It is accepting Your love with a simple, childlike faith. Joy is discovering new things about You every day. Oh, thank You, dear Jesus, for Your joy!

*The precepts of the LORD are right,*
*giving joy to the heart.*
*The commands of the LORD are radiant,*
*giving light to the eyes.*
*—PSALM 19:8*

Anne Frank wrote in her diary, "I don't think of all the misery, but of the beauty that still remains."[1] Even in the darkest circumstances, you can find joy in knowing that Jesus is by your side. How do you find joy when the circumstances around you aren't particularly joyful by worldly standards? Have you discovered any unexpected joys? Are some joys found *only* in Jesus?

_____

_____

# Gratitude Over Grumbling

Dear Jesus,

You and I both know that I complain sometimes. I guess I'm no different from anyone else, but that's the problem. You want me to be different from everyone else, so I would like to complain less often.

In summer, I complain that it's too hot. Then in winter, I complain that it's too cold. I complain when there is too much snow, not enough rain, or the wind blows too hard. I grumble when I have too much to do and when I'm bored. Jesus, I confess I even whine sometimes when I don't get my way.

I'm sorry for the many times I complain. With all that You suffered when You came to this earth, You never once complained. Even now, You give me Your best all the time—always listening, always loving, even when I'm not so lovable. Help me to be more like Paul, who gave "thanks in all circumstances" (1 Thessalonians 5:18).

Jesus, guide my eyes to see all that I have to be thankful for. Whisper in my heart that there is a better way, that there is much to be joyful about. Remind me that in all things I need to have an attitude of gratitude.

*Do everything without grumbling or arguing.*

—PHILIPPIANS 2:14

Wouldn't it be wonderful if we could be perfect like Jesus and never complain? But we aren't perfect, and we all do complain sometimes. Ask Jesus to open your eyes—and your ears—to your complaints and to forgive you for them. Strive to replace your grumbling with gratitude. In what ways can you choose to be more thankful? Are there things you can be thankful for in *any* situation?

# You Lift Me Up

Dear Jesus,

How awesome You are! You can take a day that begins badly and turn it completely around.

Jesus, You lift me up with Your perfect timing. When I need help, You send it to me in the form of a friend—or even a stranger—who shares with me Your knowledge and Your strength. When I need a respite from all the busyness in my life, You refresh me with reminders of Your presence. And when the troubles of this life drag me down, You find a way to make me smile. Jesus, You help me rise above the bad news of the day by reminding me of the good news from Your Word. You raise me above my human imperfections and make me perfect in You.

I praise You for Your love and for Your care of me. I'm so grateful that Your arms are strong enough to lift me above any barrier that life puts in my way. Thank You for being the Light that brightens my days.

*He lifted me out of the slimy pit,*
*out of the mud and mire;*
*he set my feet on a rock*
*and gave me a firm place to stand.*
—PSALM 40:2

Jesus was able to make the blind see and the lame walk, so He is certainly able to turn your day, even your life, around for the better. The same power that lifted Him from the grave can lift you above any circumstance in your life. How have you seen the power of Jesus work in your life? How does He lift you up? How can you, in turn, lift up those around you?

# Thank You for Laughter

Dear Jesus,

Thank You for making me laugh today. You opened my eyes and my ears to many funny and delightful little things. I've laughed at jokes and smiled at the simplest of pleasures. I can almost imagine that You're laughing right along with me.

I thank You for the blessings of family and friends and our times of laughter together. Our shared memories and shared moments are wonderful treasures to me, and I store them deep in my heart.

I look around me at this world and at all the delightful things You've created, and I just know You must be a God of laughter too. Why else would a squirrel be so wonderfully wiggly as it grapples for food? Why else would a giraffe's neck be so long and so spotted? So much of creation just seems designed to bring a smile—from blooming flowers to waddling mama ducks with their babies. Help me remember to look for all the many reasons to smile that You place in my day.

Thank You, Jesus, for the gift of smiles and laughter.

*"He will fill your mouth with laughter.*
*Shouts of joy will come from your lips."*

—JOB 8:21 NIRV

The theologian Martin Luther offered this humorous quote: "If you're not allowed to laugh in heaven, I don't want to go there."[1] Laughter is a wonderfully delightful part of God's creation. What has made you laugh today? What things delight you and make you smile?

# Dear Jesus, I Love You

Dear Jesus,

I love You. Your presence is like a cool breeze on a hot summer night. When I am tired and weary, You refresh me. When words sting, You soothe away my hurt. Jesus, the sweetness of Your voice calms me when I am afraid and comforts me when I mourn. You lift me above the world's noise and give me peace.

Whether I'm in a crowd of strangers or in the company of those I love, You are always there with me. I never worry about being alone. You find me when I am lost, save me from the enemy's traps, and rescue me when I'm in danger. No problem is too great for You to solve or too small to lay before You.

Oh, how wonderful You are! Powerful yet gentle, kind but strong, wise and willing. You sit on a throne at the right hand of God, yet You choose to make a home in my heart. And as great as You are, Jesus, You love *me*. I can't believe how much You love me! And Jesus—I love You, too, with all my heart.

"*I love those who love me,
and those who seek me find me.*"
—PROVERBS 8:17

Jesus loves you so much that He sacrificed His own life so you could be washed clean of sin and have eternal life. Every single moment of every day, Jesus is with you, loving you. Turn your thoughts toward Him today as you read 1 Corinthians 13:4–8. How is this definition of love reflected in Christ's love for you? Are you reflecting that same kind of love to others?

# The Little Things

Dear Jesus,

Thank You for all the little things You do, things that I too often take for granted, things like waking me in the morning and setting a new day before me—bright, fresh, and filled with hope and expectation.

Each morning You open my eyes with slivers of light slipping through my curtains, inviting me to rise and begin this day with You. All throughout the day, You surprise me with unexpected gifts of laughter, kindness, fellowship, and encouragement. When I run out of time, You whisper to me what really matters. You guide me through moments of frustration and forgive me when I lose my temper. You light my way with Your knowledge and truth. And when I dare to think I have it all figured out, You remind me that You alone are God. Then, at day's end, when I'm weary and worn, You grant me rest.

For all these little things—which really aren't so little after all—I thank You, Jesus.

*Let the morning bring me word of your unfailing love,*
*for I have put my trust in you.*
*Show me the way I should go,*
*for to you I entrust my life.*
*—PSALM 143:8*

Every moment of your life, Jesus is with you. He wakes you, guides you through your day, and gives you rest at night. Think of all the little—and not so little—things the Lord has done for you. Praise Him for being a God who draws near. How does God wake you each morning? How does He meet with you all throughout the day? How does His presence offer comfort in the dark of night?

# Your Beautiful Creation

Dear Jesus,

Your creation, Lord, is a beautiful reflection of Your might and majesty. This world, and everything You've created in it, is Your masterpiece. Forgive me for the times I allow the rush and tumble of life to become my focus—I know I miss so much. Open my eyes to see Your beauty all around me.

The works of the greatest painters, sculptors, and photographers fill the museums of the world. The works of Van Gogh, Picasso, Cézanne are amazing and priceless. But they are nothing when compared with the works of Your hands. Not even the greatest earthly artist could place the moon and the stars with such beautiful precision or sculpt the land with a word. A painter might capture a hint of the sunrise's dazzling colors, but only You can send them streaming so vividly across the sky morning by morning.

You, Lord, are the great Artist, the master Creator. You are the One who is beautiful beyond words. Thank You, dear Jesus, for blessing me with eyes to see the wonders of Your creation.

*In the beginning, the Word was already there. The Word was with God, and the Word was God. He was with God in the beginning. All things were made through him.*

—JOHN 1:1-3 NIRV

We are so much at home here on earth that we may forget what a spectacular creation earth is. Take a moment to look out your window—open your eyes to really see your corner of the world God has made. What do you see? Is there something you've never noticed before? What does God's attention to detail tell you about His creation of you?

# Those Who Serve

Dear Jesus,

Thank You for the caring hearts of those who serve. You send them, the strong and faithful, to do Your good works. They exist all around us, often unnoticed until we need them.

Police officers risk their lives to keep us peaceful and safe. Firefighters rush into the smoke and flames, putting others' lives before their own. Soldiers sacrifice their comforts and even their lives to defend our freedoms and protect us from evil. Doctors and nurses help heal the sick, chaplains comfort those who hurt, teachers teach, ministers preach, missionaries travel the world to share Your message of truth—servants, each and every one!

Dear Lord, protect those who put others before themselves. Bless them as they go about Your work. Give them the physical and emotional strength that they need for their jobs. Shield their hearts. Guide their decisions and their steps—and plant within me sweet reminders to thank them for all they do.

But most of all, Lord, I thank You—the One who sacrificed all to save me.

*Sitting down, Jesus called the Twelve and said, "Anyone who wants to be first must be the very last, and the servant of all."*

—MARK 9:35

Do you remember to thank God for all those who serve in your life—the crossing guard at school, the police officer directing traffic, the teenage neighbor who was there when you needed a helping hand? Jesus' helpers are all around you, meeting your everyday needs. How many people work to serve you each day? Is there something you can do to serve those who serve others?

# Reflections on Gratitude

# Reflections on Gratitude

# Jesus, I Need You . . . When I Feel Heartache

# Brighter Future

Dear Jesus,

It's so easy to let myself be haunted by the past. Old memories of not-so-good times swirl around in my mind. Why is it so hard to let go? I have forgiven past transgressions, but I haven't forgotten. Perhaps I never will. Lord, help me at least to set them aside and not dwell on them.

You've forgiven my sins, and You want me to forgive the sins of others. I think I've done that, but the pain remains. I still hurt. Heal me, Lord. I want to let go. Instead of being consumed by a hurtful past, I want to focus on a brighter future.

Today, I will turn my thoughts toward You and what lies ahead. And whenever the past rises up to haunt me, I will send it away with thoughts of Your good plans for me. Jesus, open the door to my future today. Hold my hand, and help me to walk through the door with You.

*Brothers and sisters, I do not consider myself yet to have taken hold of it. But one thing I do: Forgetting what is behind and straining toward what is ahead.*

—PHILIPPIANS 3:13

Yesterday's pain serves only to dim Christ's light today. Give past hurts to Him, and allow His light to shine brightly in your heart. Ask Jesus to heal your wounds and set you on the path to an abundant future. Read Romans 5:3–5. How might God be using past hurts to shape you for His abundant life? What signs of that abundant life do you see blooming in your life today?

# Fitting In

Dear Jesus,

I'm feeling cut off from the world. Everyone else seems to fit like a piece in a puzzle while I'm feeling pushed to the side, forgotten and misunderstood. I've tried to reach out, but it's not working right now. I feel like a square peg in a round hole.

I need the warmth, encouragement, and love of friends right now. And while I know that I am never truly alone—that You're always with me—I feel isolated. In my mind, I know this feeling is temporary. But in my heart? I just don't see the way to go. Show me my place, where to fit in—in a way that honors You and with people who also love You.

Jesus, I am so grateful that You are always here with me in my heart, guiding me and loving me. Friends may leave and they may fail me, but You never leave me and You never let me down. You understand my thoughts and feelings, my hopes and dreams. You know exactly where I'm supposed to fit in, and You know exactly who my friends should be. Lead me to them, Lord. And until then, draw me closer to You.

*There is a friend who sticks closer than a brother.*

—PROVERBS 18:24

There may be times when you feel as if you don't fit in—that happens to everyone at one time or another. Feeling uncomfortable with the company you keep can lead to loneliness, but Jesus wants you to remember that He is always with you. Even so, Jesus can use these times when you feel lonely to pull you closer to Him. How can you use times of aloneness to draw nearer to Him? In what ways is Jesus your forever and faithful friend?

# Losing a Loved One

Dear Jesus,

Someone I love has died, and my heart is broken. I want to be strong, knowing that this person is free from suffering. My loved one is with You in heaven now, well and strong. Still, my heart aches.

By faith, I know that we will see each other again. But I long to see, to hug, to laugh together just once more.

In my sadness, I've asked You why. Why did my loved one have to suffer? Why did death come so soon? I know Your answers are beyond my understanding, but maybe someday, when we meet face-to-face, You will share them with me.

Jesus, when Your friend Lazarus died, You wept with sorrow. So I know You understand my pain as I weep for the one I love. Please comfort me, dear Jesus. Take the ache in my heart and ease it with Your gentle love. Wrap me up warmly in Your embrace until my broken heart is mended.

*Where, O death, is your victory?*
*Where, O death, is your sting?*

—1 CORINTHIANS 15:55

When Jesus walked here on earth, He experienced every heartache the devil could throw at Him—so He understands our every sorrow and sadness. You have a Savior who can comfort you because He knows firsthand what suffering is. How do Jesus' experiences help you know that He understands your sorrow? How might your own sorrows help you understand and comfort others?

# Safe Place

Dear Jesus,

My friend and I were so close, but then things changed. I'm not even sure how, and I definitely don't know why. She chose one path, and I chose another. And now she's said things, done things—I just feel so betrayed. Oh, Jesus! It hurts so much.

I trusted her with my deepest secrets, my deepest fears, and she's using them against me. It makes me so angry. I know I need to forgive her, but I need Your help. Help me let go of these hard feelings and pray for her.

So, Lord, please reach out to her, draw her to You. Whatever hurt she's harboring, I pray that you would heal it. I pray that you would bless her life with goodness and that you would draw both of us closer to You. Help us each to see the wrongs we've done and to make them right. Forgive her, Lord, and forgive me. And thank You, Lord, for being the ever-true friend I can always run to. You are my safe place in the storm.

*The Lord is my rock and my place of safety.*
*He is the God who saves me.*
*My God is my rock. I go to him for safety.*
*He is like a shield to me. He's the power that*
*saves me. He's my place of safety.*
—PSALM 18:2 NIRV

Betrayal—by a friend, a loved one, a coworker—is a painful and shattering experience. What can you do? Lean hard into Jesus and allow Him to help you. And then forgive and move on. Is there someone you have yet to forgive? Think of all that Jesus has forgiven you for—and the truth that if you refuse to forgive another, then God will not forgive you (Matthew 6:14–15). How does that make you feel about withholding your forgiveness?

# Seek and Save

Dear Jesus,

Someone I care about has chosen to walk away from You, and it's breaking my heart. He doesn't think he needs You, but You are the greatest need in his life right now. He is like the lost sheep in the parable. He has left You and gone his way. Lord, You tell me that You go out searching for the sheep who are lost—search for him, Lord. Soften his heart, and help him to return to You. Show me how I can help. Give me the right words to say.

Jesus, as much as I treasure him, You treasure him so much more. You want only the very best for him, and I know that You're working in his life to bring him back to You. And so I praise You, Lord, for being a God who goes out to seek and save the lost.

*"Suppose one of you has a hundred sheep and loses one of them. Doesn't he leave the ninety-nine in the open country and go after the lost sheep until he finds it? And when he finds it, he joyfully puts it on his shoulders and goes home."*

—LUKE 15:4-6

To see someone you care about turn away from Jesus is heart-breaking. But remember, no one wants that person to turn back to God more than Jesus. Pray and ask Him to work in that person's heart and life. Ask Him to show you how you can make a difference. Whom do you need to be praying for, interceding for, today? Make a list, and commit yourself to praying for those people every day.

# Words Can Hurt Me

Dear Jesus,

I confess to You that I have gossiped. I have said things about others that I would never say in their presence—and should never have said at all. And Jesus, when I did it, I never gave it a second thought. But now gossip is the only thing on my mind because I am a victim of it.

Lord, I am learning that shameful words wound deeply. Like arrows, they pierce the heart and tear into the soul. And when unkind words are spoken by a loved one, they hurt even more. They sting, shattering trust into a million tiny pieces.

How can I be angry with the one who hurt me when I have hurt others in the same way? My pain is shadowed by feelings of guilt. Forgive me, Lord, and heal me.

Jesus, I have learned a lesson in this heartache. And with Your help, I will watch the words that come from my lips so that they will never again cause anyone to hurt.

*The words of the reckless pierce like swords,*
*but the tongue of the wise brings healing.*
—PROVERBS 12:18

Are you guilty of gossip? Have words ever hurt you? The pain caused by reckless words can often wound more deeply and hurt longer than physical pain. The old saying—"Sticks and stones may break my bones, but words will never hurt me"—is a lie. Read Psalm 141:3 and Proverbs 16:24. Then write out a prayer asking God to help you always live—and speak—according to *these* words.

# A New Calling

Dear Jesus,

My life has been filled with heartache. You and I have spent many long nights together discussing the reasons why, and from our conversations I have learned that *why* doesn't matter. What does matter is how I react.

Jesus, through years of heartache, You have molded my spirit. You have refined me, tempered me, made me strong. Your mercy has brought softness into hard places and caused me to reach outside of myself to meet the needs and soothe the hurts of others. You've opened my eyes to the pain all around me and reminded me that I'm not alone in my suffering.

So perhaps I've already received Your answer to my endlessly asking, "Why?" It's so I can help others—comfort as I have been comforted, lend an understanding ear, aid because I now know how to help. I can do those things because of all I've endured—a sweet blessing from bitter times. This blessing prompts me to say, "Thank You, Lord" for bringing goodness from all I've endured.

*My brothers and sisters, you will face all kinds of trouble. When you do, think of it as pure joy. Your faith will be tested. You know that when this happens it will produce in you the strength to continue. And you must allow this strength to finish its work. Then you will be all you should be. You will have everything you need.*

—JAMES 1:2–4 NIRV

Not only can Jesus ease your pain, but oftentimes He uses it to lead you to a new calling. Ask many volunteers, and they'll tell you that they experienced a heartache that led them to serve others. Consider Romans 8:28 as you look back over your own past heartaches. Can you now see how God has used them for your good? How might you use those experiences for the good of others?

# Do You Weep?

Dear Jesus,

Do You weep when You see what we've done? Does it break Your heart? Our earth, this place that You created in flawless, peaceful beauty, has become swathed in sin. It's sad—so very shameful. And we've got no one to blame but ourselves.

Sometimes I wonder why we continue to make such poor choices. You give us the freedom to choose. We can choose to follow You and make the world a better place, or we can choose sin. So why do we continuously choose sin when it leads only to heartache? *Why do I so often choose sin?*

I'm grateful, Lord, that You haven't given up on us—that You haven't given up on me. You suffered such pain and anguish on the cross so that those You love will have eternal life. And You continue to love us in spite of our sinful imperfections.

Jesus, You are my Savior, the One who brings peace in the midst of earthly storms. I need You. Forgive me. Cleanse me. Make me new. Lord Jesus, please make me more like You.

*Again and again they tested God.*
*They made the Holy One of Israel sad and angry.*
—PSALM 78:41 NIRV

We read in Genesis 6:6, "The Lord was very sad that he had made human beings on the earth. His heart was filled with pain" (NIRV). Have you ever considered that God's heart can be broken, just as yours can? We know that Jesus wept; the Bible tells us so. What are the sins in this world—in your own life—that break your heart? What can you do about them?

# Pleasing You

Dear Jesus,

It seems that no matter what I do, no matter how hard I try, my efforts are never good enough. It makes me want to stop trying. Some days I feel so discouraged that I can barely get out of bed to face another day.

I try my best, Lord, I really do. I try to serve and help and do what's needed, but it just doesn't seem to be enough. What does it take to please the people in my life? Oh . . . but maybe that's the problem: I'm trying to please people when I should be more worried about pleasing You.

Lord, remind me—again and again—that I need to place You first in my life. When I do that, all these other things will fall into place. Pleasing people isn't important—it's pleasing You that matters! Teach me to seek to please You first. Restore me, and take this sadness away. I am Your creation, and You love me and find delight in me. You created me with a purpose and a plan. Lead me to that purpose; guide me with Your plan.

I praise You, Lord, for listening to my cries. I know You hear me, I know You are faithful, and I know You're already working out the answer to this prayer. Thank You!

*The Spirit of God has made me;*
*the breath of the Almighty gives me life.*

—JOB 33:4

You may become depressed when you expect too much of yourself or when you put too much emphasis on pleasing others. When your self-esteem tumbles, remember that God made you—fearfully and wonderfully—in His image. Read Galatians 1:10, and ask yourself if your efforts are more about pleasing people than pleasing God. Now read Matthew 6:33. Does this verse change the way you think about pleasing the people in your life? What changes might you need to make?

# Nothing Can Harm Me

Dear Jesus,

I believe that whatever happens, You will lift me high above the pain. Nothing can truly harm me—the eternal part of me—because I am Yours and You are with me. You are my fortress and my shield.

When the storm rushes over me, when the flood threatens—water rising, swirling, pulling me under—You reach down and save me. You set my feet on the high ground and shelter me safely beneath Your wings. When lightning flashes and thunder roars, You whisper, "Do not be afraid."

The road is long, Lord, but when I grow weary, You carry me. You never leave my side. We're on this journey together, and I know You will not desert me or fail me. When sorrow overtakes me, You dry my tears. You give me courage not to give up. You are the source of my strength.

You know where and how this journey will end, and You remind me that the sadness and pain are not forever. Dear Jesus, I could not do this without You. Thank You for holding me, for helping me, for healing me. I love You so much!

*He heals the brokenhearted*
*and binds up their wounds.*
—PSALM 147:3

When sorrow breaks your heart wide open, let Jesus in. He will not only heal you, but He will also make you whole. Read Psalm 3:3–5. Have you seen these truths played out in your own life or in the lives of others? How so? In what ways does it help you to know that the Lord is both your shield and your sustainer?

# Reflections on Heartache

# Reflections on Heartache

# Jesus, I Need Your . . . Comfort

# You Are My Refuge

Dear Jesus,

Thank You for providing security in an insecure world. You warned that "nation will rise against nation, and kingdom against kingdom. There will be earthquakes in various places, and famines. These are the beginning of birth pains" (Mark 13:8). All of this and more will signal Your coming. But You also said, "Do not be alarmed" (Mark 13:7). Jesus, when things seem to be spiraling out of control, I trust that You are in control.

In this ever-changing world, You never change. Every promise You have made, I know You will keep. Whatever happens, no matter how disturbing, Your love will see me through. And because You are always with me, I will not be afraid.

Jesus, when the world seems dark, You give me light. You are strength in weakness and hope in despair. Your precepts never change, nor does Your purpose. You are always holy, just, and right. Most of all, You are there—shielding, protecting, comforting, and reassuring me. I am safe in Your presence. Thank You, Jesus, for being my refuge.

*"Do not fear, for I have redeemed you;*
*I have summoned you by name; you are mine."*
—ISAIAH 43:1

Today's world can be a frightening place. Everywhere you look, there seems to be disaster, tragedy, and bad news. But as a Christian, you have the gift of knowing that God is your refuge. In fact, God is referred to as your refuge more than forty times in the book of Psalms. Look up the word *refuge*, and write its definition here. How has God been your refuge?

_____

_____

_____

_____

_____

_____

_____

_____

_____

_____

_____

_____

_____

_____

_____

_____

# Watch Over Those I Love

Dear Jesus,

I come to You in prayer today asking You to watch over the ones I love. This world is such a worrisome place—with accidents, illnesses, and evil. I worry, Lord. I know I shouldn't. I know that You are watching over them and that You are always with them. But still, I worry.

I love them so, Lord. And as much as I love them, I know that You love them even more. So I entrust them to You, to Your love, to Your watchful care. Please keep them safe in this unsafe world. Bless them with wisdom, and guide them with Your light. But most of all, dear Jesus, keep them always, ever close to You. Make them hungry for Your teaching and for Your Word.

Dear Jesus, I thank You for the gift of these ones I love, and for the joy they bring to my life. Help me not to worry about them because You are always watching over them. Wrap Your arms around them—and me.

I love You, Jesus. Thank You for watching over us.

*The LORD will watch over your coming and going*
*both now and forevermore.*
*—PSALM 121:8*

When it comes to the loved ones in our lives, we want to protect them and keep them safe. But it's so easy for the desire to protect to turn into worry. Entrust your loved ones to God; remember He loves them more than you could ever imagine. Read the words of Psalm 121. List all the different ways the Lord watches over and protects His people. Do these words lessen your worry?

# You and Me

Dear Jesus,

I love it when we spend time together, just the two of us, You and me. You have this amazing ability to lead me to places where there are no distractions. Sometimes it's to enjoy a quiet walk together; other times, You meet me at the kitchen table for a cup of tea. Though my eyes can't see You, my heart can. I feel You all around me, and I hear Your voice in my ear. I get up early to meet You in the quiet of the morning, and so often Yours is the last voice I hear before I fall asleep at night.

The time I spend with You is precious to me, Jesus. You are Lord of all—and just knowing how much You love me makes me feel so special. I'm honored that You *want* to spend time with me, to know me, and stay by my side as You guide me through life. Whether it's to share in some small pleasure or to conquer a roadblock in my way, You meet me wherever I am. We go through life together, my God and me, the best of friends.

Thank You, dear Jesus. Thank You for this time You spend with me.

*Come near to God and he will come near to you.*

—JAMES 4:8

Jesus' voice is most clear when you spend time alone with Him. That time doesn't have to follow a set formula. Simply be still with Him, read His Word, and ponder what it says. Listen for His voice, praise Him, talk to Him—any of these things or all of these things. This time should be about your relationship, not a ritual. In what ways do you spend time with your Savior and friend? If you're not spending that time with Him, commit to doing so, and write that commitment here.

# Quiet Time

Dear Jesus,

Thank You for quiet times. I love the calm rituals before sleep—the cup of tea, the quiet conversations, the slower pace at the end of the day. And I love slipping between the covers and resting in Your love. A sense of peace surrounds me—a peace that comes from You, from Your presence.

Jesus, I'm grateful for those quiet times that I spend with You: praying, praising You, meditating on Your Word. Those times are so special, so important to me. They ground me and remind me of all that is truly important. It is in those quiet times that I feel closest to You. And even in the rush of my busy life, somehow You carve out a quiet moment so we can spend time together.

I think of David's words in Psalm 23: "He leads me beside quiet waters, he refreshes my soul" (vv. 2–3). That's what You do for me, Jesus. You refresh me in the quiet moments of my day. Thank You.

"In repentance and rest is your salvation,
in quietness and trust is your strength."
—ISAIAH 30:15

Jesus adds peace to our lives. He brings gentleness and love to our days, refreshing us and giving us sweet rest. But quiet time rarely happens by accident; it must be sought out and fiercely defended. Several times in the Bible, we see Jesus slipping away from the crowds for quiet time alone with His Father. Does knowing that even Jesus needed quiet time affect the importance you assign to your own quiet times? Why do you think Jesus needed time alone with God?

# All Around

Dear Jesus,

You are all around me. You are the joy in every happy ending. And You are the courage, the comfort, and the strength in even those endings that aren't so happy. Jesus, I see You in hospitals, guiding the doctors and nurses as they serve the sick. You are in the smiles of those who visit the nursing homes, in the hands of those who serve meals to the poor, and in the hearts of those who shelter the homeless. Wherever there is hope—wherever there is love, care, and compassion—Jesus, You are there.

I find You in the laughter of children and in the hugs and kisses of those I love. You're there in the warmth of friendship and in the kindness of strangers.

I hear You in the exuberant joy of Sunday morning songs and in the well-chosen words from Your teachings. You are in every prayer and in every met need. But my favorite place to find You, Lord Jesus, is in my heart—this day and always. Thank You for staying close to me.

"You will seek me and find me when you
seek me with all your heart."

—JEREMIAH 29:13

In the busyness of your days, remember Jesus. If you look for Him—not only with your eyes, but with your heart—then you'll find Him all around you. He is in every good thing and in every act of kindness. Look for Jesus in likely and unlikely places. Notice Him—He's there. How many different places do you see Him at work? How many different ways does He reveal His presence to you?

# Grant Me Peace

Dear Jesus,

You are the Prince of Peace, and I need peace today. Will You help me find it? You know the problem that I'm struggling with. It makes me feel anxious, and my mind is filled with worry. I don't know what to do. I hate being locked up with this storm that's inside me. Dear Jesus, I need You.

I remember that Paul said, "Do not be anxious about anything, but in every situation, by prayer and petition, with thanksgiving, present your requests to God. And the peace of God, which transcends all understanding, will guard your hearts and your minds in Christ Jesus" (Philippians 4:6–7).

It sounds so simple, Lord. If I leave my problem at Your feet, and if I ask You to grant me peace, You will. But it's not so simple for me to do. I believe, Lord. I truly do believe that if I keep my mind fixed on You, this anxious feeling will go away. Help my unbelief.

Guard my heart and my mind, Lord Jesus, and fill me with Your peace.

"The LORD turn his face toward you and give you peace."

—NUMBERS 6:26

Finding Your peace in Jesus takes practice. It means learning to give all your cares to Him—and not snatching them back to worry over some more. It means resting in His love and trusting that He'll work things out for your good. Start your path to finding peace by answering these questions: Has worrying ever truly helped you? What would happen if you stopped worrying? What would your days look like if you surrendered them all to Jesus? And how would having Jesus' peace change you?

_____

_____

_____

_____

_____

_____

_____

_____

_____

_____

_____

_____

# Comfort My Friend

Dear Jesus,

My friend is hurting. You know what happened, Lord—even better than I do. So I come to You today asking that You help my friend.

I don't know how to help; I only know to pray. She has pulled away from me, from everyone, really. When she has to be around me, she acts as if nothing has happened. If I offer condolences or help, she refuses and replies, "I'm fine." But Jesus, I know that she is not fine. She is hurting, and I want to comfort and help her. I want her to know that I and many others are here for her.

If I can't help, Jesus, I *know* that You can. You are with her during the darkest, loneliest times, and I know that You will never leave her alone. Open her heart to You so she can feel Your love. Comfort her and dry her tears. And Jesus, if there is any way I can help, please show me how. I love my friend, and she needs You.

*When Jesus entered Capernaum, a Roman commander came to him. He asked Jesus for help. "Lord," he said, "my servant lies at home and can't move. He is suffering terribly." Jesus said, "Shall I come and heal him?"*

—MATTHEW 8:5-7 NIRV

Some people have a difficult time accepting help from others, especially when they're hurting. In the worst times, they may even avoid their friends and withdraw deep inside themselves. Sometimes you might feel that there is little you can do to help. But there is something! You can bring that person before the Lord in prayer. In fact, God's Word urges us to pray for others (1 Timothy 2:1). How will you pray for those in your life who are hurting?

# When I Need Rest

Dear Jesus,

I am so tired, and I know I need to rest. But this world doesn't encourage rest. It almost seems to view the need for rest as a weakness. So I thank You for teaching me that it's not only important to rest, but it's also okay to rest.

When You lived on earth, You would sometimes slip away from the crowds and even from Your closest disciples to spend time alone with Your Father. You took time to refresh and recharge Your body and soul so You could then get back to work. Yours is the example I must remember to follow whenever I feel weary.

I am reminded of Your words: "Come to me, all you who are weary and burdened, and I will give you rest" (Matthew 11:28). Help me not to feel guilty for stepping away, but instead to look forward to going off alone with You to pray and read the Bible. I want to meditate on Your goodness. I want to lie down to sleep knowing You are with me.

Thank You, Jesus, for being my place of refreshment and renewal. Thank You for being a quiet place of peace when I need to rest.

*Then Jesus said to his apostles, "Come with me by yourselves to a quiet place. You need to get some rest."*

—MARK 6:31 NIRV

Rest is so very important but so very easy to neglect. But even Jesus, as busy as He was, made time to rest. True rest means more than simply resting your body with sleep or resting your mind by settling down with a good book; true rest is also finding rest for your soul. The Bible reminds us to "rest in the LORD" (Psalm 37:7 KJV). What does it mean to you to "rest in the LORD"? Do you make time for that kind of rest? If not, how might you find that time? How might it restore you?

# When I Am Sick

Dear Jesus,

I need You. My body is sick and hurting, and I just feel awful. I can't sleep; my mind is so full of anxious thoughts. I need Your healing and Your comfort.

Dear Jesus, I come to You empty-handed. I'm so weak that I have nothing left to give except my love and my trust. I believe that You can heal me. Will You, Lord? I place myself in Your hands because I know You have a plan for me, and I know it's a perfect plan—even if it might be different from my plan. Maybe You won't heal me on this side of heaven—maybe Your plan is for the perfect healing of heaven. But maybe You will bless me with earthly, physical healing—and that is my hope.

Help me to remain faithful in the midst of this illness. I know You're with me, and You're watching over me night and day. I believe in Your love for me, and I feel the comfort of Your presence. Help me fix my thoughts on You instead of on this sickness. Fill me with Your strength and Your courage. I love You, Lord, and I thank You for loving me.

*Praise be to the God and Father of our Lord Jesus Christ, the Father of compassion and the God of all comfort, who comforts us in all our troubles, so that we can comfort those in any trouble with the comfort we ourselves receive from God.*

—2 CORINTHIANS 1:3–4

Illness—especially a serious, prolonged illness—is a true test of faith. Physical discomfort and anxious thoughts make it difficult to focus on Christ's love. But don't let the enemy use illness to rob you of your faith. Write out all the things that are troubling and worrying you, all the things that hurt. Then deliberately and intentionally, in writing, entrust each one to Jesus' care.

# The Comforts of Home

Dear Jesus,

As I sit here gazing out my window, I begin to think of all the little comforts You bring to me, to my home. So often it's the little things that comfort me most, things like waking up to warm sunshine streaming through the bedroom window, the familiar sounds of the world outside, the aroma of freshly brewed coffee, even that old creak in the floor. They all remind me that there's no place like home. Whether I'm sitting down to a meal in my own kitchen or slipping into bed at the end of the day, I feel the warm comfort of Your presence all around me.

Jesus, You are always here with me, watching over me, protecting me, and providing for me. You've blessed me with this home—not only with the safety of its walls, but also with the shelter of Your love. You provide food for my table and sustenance for my soul. You chase away the darkness with Your light. And You even comfort me with Your grace and mercy on those days when the world outside seems too harsh to face.

Thank You, Lord, for my home here, but most of all thank You for my home with You.

*Whoever dwells in the shelter of the Most High*
*will rest in the shadow of the Almighty.*
—PSALM 91:1

Have you given thought to how Jesus makes your house a home? Look around for all the little things you might have missed or taken for granted. Some people refer to these blessings as creature comforts, but in truth, they are Christ comforts! What are some of your favorite Christ comforts? And because your home is a blessing from God, how can you use it to draw others to Him?

# Reflections on Comfort

# Reflections on Comfort

# Jesus, I Need Your . . . Grace

# That Difficult Person

Dear Jesus,

I need Your help. Someone is making my life difficult. I have tried to be kind and patient—You know I have, Lord. But there have been times when I've lost my temper—You know that too. I've said unkind things and thought even worse things. Our relationship needs healing; it needs You.

Jesus, show me what to do. I pray for You to step in and make this right. Teach me, Lord. How would You handle this person? Please take away these feelings of anger and hurt and replace them with grace and love.

"Seventy times seven": That's what You said to Peter when he asked how many times he should forgive the one who sinned against him. Am I capable of forgiving that many times? Oh, but how many times have You forgiven me? Soften my heart, Lord, and help me forgive as You have forgiven me.

If anyone can mend this relationship, Jesus, it is You. Guide my every word and every action with Your perfect love. I need You, Jesus. *We* need You.

*If it is possible, as far as it depends on you, live at peace with everyone.*

−ROMANS 12:18

At some point in your life, you'll encounter a difficult person—someone who, no matter what you do, makes your life miserable. When you run into such a person, call on Jesus. He understands and will know just how to help. As you think about that difficult person, ask yourself if you've contributed to the strain. Are there things for which you need to seek forgiveness? Come up with at least one thing you can do to bless that person's life—and then do it.

# Learning Patience

Dear Jesus,

This world moves so fast, and I feel as if I'm supposed to keep up with it. I'm finding it hard to slow down, to wait, to be still. I get so impatient when something is out of my control and I'm forced to wait for a resolution. It's like being stuck in a traffic jam where I can't go forward and I can't go back—I'm just stuck.

But Jesus, You are always so patient with me. You are patient when You teach me. And You are patient when it takes me a while to learn—because so often You have to teach me the same lesson over and over again. You are patient when my faith in You falters, and You are even patient with my impatience! I want to be more like You, Lord. When things get in my way, I want to be able to say, and to truly mean it, "Lord, I know You've got this. You'll work it out. I'll just slow down, be calm, and wait on You."

I need You, Jesus. Please help me to calm down, to slow down, even to be still sometimes. Lead me to be more patient.

*Wait for the LORD;*
*be strong and take heart*
*and wait for the LORD.*
*—PSALM 27:14*

Waiting is hard work, often harder than the work itself. So when life throws a roadblock in your way, it's the perfect opportunity to practice patience. When you are forced to wait, think of it as a gift, as if God is saying to you, "Not yet. I know what's ahead." Is there an area of your life in which you need to practice more patience? How might you choose to see obstacles as opportunities to practice patience?

# The Power of Community

Dear Jesus,

Thank You for my friends at church. I'm so grateful that You've blessed me with a community of fellow believers who love You as I do and who encourage me to love You even more.

Jesus, You have taught me that there is power in this community of mine. We pray and study Your Word together, and we enjoy finding ways to show others how much You love them. Together we are stronger in our faith and are better able to share You with the world. You watch over us and make us aware of needs that we might otherwise miss. And when You reveal a need, You give us the resources we need to meet it. Faithfully You lead us as Your disciples, giving us a heart for people both near and far.

Jesus, You have shown me that I am one piece of a big, beautiful puzzle. When You put me together with these friends—these brothers and sisters—our faith interlocks to create a bigger and even more beautiful picture of how we can serve You.

Thank You, Jesus, for my family of believers! Please continue to bless us and guide us.

*So in Christ we, though many, form one body,*
*and each member belongs to all the others.*

—ROMANS 12:5

When Jesus lived on earth, He didn't carry out His ministry alone. He enlisted disciples to help Him. And today, Jesus' community of disciples continues to grow. In churches throughout the world, believers gather together to share God's Word, pray, and help meet the needs of others. How does your church bless you and help meet your spiritual needs? How do you feel about those who say they don't need a church to worship God? Do you agree?

# Loving Everyone

Dear Jesus,

Sometimes it's really hard to love people, especially when You ask me to love those who hate You and do evil things. I know *You* love them, but I struggle to follow Your example. Please show me how can I hate the evil while still loving those who hate You.

Jesus, when You were beaten, mocked, and crucified, You could have rained down wrath from heaven, but You didn't. Instead, You asked God to forgive Your enemies because they didn't know what they were doing. That is pure love. Fill me with that kind of love.

Jesus, You are always in my heart, guiding me and leading me to be more like You. And for that reason, I must pray for those who hate You and do evil things. I don't love what they do, Lord—but I want them to know You. Please, Lord Jesus, open their eyes to see You and their hearts to accept You. They need You so much . . . and so, Lord, do I.

> "You have heard that it was said, 'Love your neighbor and hate your enemy.' But I tell you, love your enemies and pray for those who persecute you."
>
> —MATTHEW 5:43–44

Love doesn't mean that you accept acts of hatred and evil, but love does require that you pray for those most in need of salvation. Consider Paul. He didn't begin life as a disciple of Christ; in fact, there was a time when Paul—then known as Saul—hated Christ. Read Acts 9:1–19 to discover how he changed. How might you be an Ananias to a Saul in your life?

# Childlike Faith

Dear Jesus,

The questions and comments of children make me think. They aren't afraid to see the wonder in this world, and they aren't afraid to ask, "Why?" They ask silly, simple things like these: "Why do zebras have stripes?" "Why do bees buzz?" "How come dogs bark instead of meow?" They ask questions we grown-ups don't know how to answer. But when we say, "Because God made them that way," these trusting children say, "Oh, okay." They accept that answer. It's good enough for them. Shouldn't it be good enough for us too?

I wish that I had that kind of childlike faith. When I ask, "Why?" You so often answer, "Because I made you that way" or "Because that's the way I need it to be" or even just "Trust Me." I confess, Lord, that I often want a different answer, a more detailed and concrete answer. It's difficult for me to accept by faith that some things just are the way they are.

Jesus, I know You have an answer to every question—I just may not always understand it. Help me accept Your answers with the trusting faith of a child.

"As the heavens are higher than the earth,
so are my ways higher than your ways
and my thoughts than your thoughts."
—ISAIAH 55:9

When you ask Jesus a question, He expects you to trust that His answer is perfectly right in every way. So when He answers your "Why?" with "Trust Me," then He wants you to do just that. Trust Him with a childlike faith—though that's not always easy to do. Read Jeremiah 29:11 and Isaiah 55:9, and weave them into a prayer declaring your trust in Jesus' answers for you.

# Angels in Disguise

Dear Jesus,

I'm so thankful You are in my life. And I know that You are truly *in* my life because in my times of greatest need, You send people to help me. Some are family, friends, and neighbors, but many are strangers. I call them "angels," for they have gifted me with Your heavenly help. They stop whatever they're doing to help, selflessly and tirelessly.

I see Your angels everywhere, Jesus—ordinary people sent out to meet the needs of others, to love with Your love, to comfort with Your comfort, to strengthen with Your strength. Sometimes they know they're on a mission to help You, but so often You prefer to work quietly through them, leaving them unaware of the difference they've made in someone's life.

These "angels" among us tend to shy away from thanks and praise. But You know who they are, Jesus, these helpers of Yours. You know the impact they have. Bless them, and show them how much they are needed and loved.

*Do not forget to show hospitality to strangers,*
*for by so doing some people have shown*
*hospitality to angels without knowing it.*

—HEBREWS 13:2

Real angels do exist, but more often the Lord uses human helpers to meet specific needs. He works through missionaries, pastors, community leaders, neighbors, strangers—He works through you! Whenever you act with kindness or offer encouragement, Jesus is using you to meet someone's need. How have God's earthly "angels" impacted your life? What can you do today to offer heavenly help to someone in need?

---

# Rewards of Believing

Dear Jesus,

I believe that You exist, that You are real, and that You reward those who earnestly seek You. You reward me with peace in the midst of chaos, and You bless me with contentment when I struggle with worldly wants. You mend my brokenness and replace my despair with hope. You teach me patience in times of adversity and sustain me with courage when I'm afraid. You are loyal to me when others are not. Your love dries my tears, and Your strength lifts me above the circumstances of this world. I want for nothing because You give me all I need. When I call out to You, You hear me, You answer, and You bless me with Your very best.

Though I am so undeserving, You reward me with endless and unbelievable grace. Because I believe in You, because I know You are my Savior, death holds no meaning for me. My life is eternal with Your promise of heaven.

Jesus, You are my all—my best reward.

*And without faith it is impossible to please God, because anyone who comes to him must believe that he exists and that he rewards those who earnestly seek him.*

—HEBREWS 11:6

Knowing Jesus will bring you joy—a joy that transcends your circumstances. He is always faithful to those who believe in Him and earnestly seek Him. What is it that makes you believe Jesus is real? How will you seek Him today? Jesus promised to reward those who earnestly seek Him. How has He rewarded you?

# Guilt Versus Grace

Dear Jesus,

Every day You shower Your grace on me, blessing me in ways I know I don't deserve. But sometimes when You bless me with something wonderful, I feel a pang of guilt. I look at all the people suffering around me, and I ask myself, *Why am I—such a sinner—so blessed while others suffer so much?* There is still that part of me that believes I must earn Your grace.

Jesus, I know You loved me even before I loved You. Your love is perfect and unconditional—no strings attached. When I decided to trust in You, to follow You, it was Your merciful grace that saved me from sin and gave me eternal life. And it's still Your grace that blesses me every day with things I know I don't deserve. How can I ever repay You? I struggle to accept that Your grace is a gift, freely given.

Jesus, I do accept Your gifts, and I will do so with praise and thanksgiving, not guilt. Thank You for this grace I so desperately need.

*But grow in the grace and knowledge of our Lord and Savior Jesus Christ. To him be glory both now and forever! Amen.*

—2 PETER 3:18

Grace is not earned; rather, it's God's gift to you when you choose to follow Him. Paul explained in Ephesians 2:8–9: "For it is by grace you have been saved, through faith—and this is not from yourselves, it is the gift of God—not by works, so that no one can boast." And while you cannot earn God's grace, you can thank Him for it. Read Psalm 103, and then rewrite it in your own words as a prayer praising God for His grace in your life.

# What a Mess

Dear Jesus,

I've made a mess of things. I've said and done things without seeking Your will. Now I've made everything so much worse.

The situation was not mine; it was hers to work through. My intentions were good, Jesus. I stepped in wanting to help, but I went about it all wrong. I betrayed her confidence, shared her secret, and brought someone else into a private situation. I gave advice that was unsolicited, unwanted, and wrong. Now I am suffering from a broken relationship and a guilty conscience.

Jesus, I have asked her for forgiveness, and now I ask for Yours. Please forgive me for not turning to You for guidance. Forgive me for barging into a situation that was private between You and her. Forgive me for thinking that I knew how to help better than You. Please, Jesus, take this sin and guilt away from me. And thank You for forgiving me.

*"Though your sins are like scarlet,*
*they shall be as white as snow;*
*though they are red as crimson,*
*they shall be like wool."*
—ISAIAH 1:18

It's so important to talk to God about solving a problem *before* you dive in. Acting impulsively—even with good intentions— can lead to a mess. But mercy and forgiveness are wonderful parts of God's grace. When you've done something wrong, run to Him instead of away from Him. Is there something you need to be forgiven for? Psalm 51 is David's plea for forgiveness. How does it echo your own needs?

# Faith and Grace

Dear Jesus,

You have taught me that faith and grace are not two separate things; rather, they go hand in hand. For whenever I put my faith in You, I am rewarded with Your grace—and Your grace is always sufficient to meet my needs.

But so often grace doesn't come in the ways I expect. Sometimes it comes quickly, a surprise ending to a test of faith. Other times, it flows slowly and surely, sustaining me day by day. Whether it is a basic need—like food, clothing, or shelter—or a bigger need—like mending a broken relationship, overcoming a financial burden, or dealing with an illness—I know You always hear my prayers. And I know You are already working to answer them. Let my faith be unshaken as I rely on and wait for Your perfect will, as I trust Your abundant grace.

I have learned, often the hard way, to trust You fully and completely. You are always faithful, Lord. And when I put my trust in You, Your grace does not fail me. It is always enough.

*But he said to me, "My grace is sufficient for you,*
*for my power is made perfect in weakness."*

—2 CORINTHIANS 12:9

Charles Spurgeon once said, "Soar back through all your own experiences. Think of how the Lord has led you in the wilderness and has fed and clothed you every day. . . . Think of how the Lord's grace has been sufficient for you in all your troubles."[1] How has God blessed you with His grace? How do you offer that same grace to others?

# Reflections on Grace

# Reflections on Grace

Jesus, I Need You . . .
When I Feel
Disappointment

# This Mixed-Up World

Dear Jesus,

I'm frustrated with this mixed-up world. Everything seems turned upside down. What You've declared to be evil and wrong is often considered to be right and good. There are even those who change Your Word so it fits what they want to do and who they want You to be. You're not welcome in many schools and public places anymore. If You knock, so many doors are locked up tight. People hurt each other, Jesus. Everywhere I look I see fighting and discord, and bad news outweighs the good.

You mean so much to me. I want the whole world to know You and follow You. I do my best to tell others about Your goodness, but sometimes I feel as if it isn't doing any good. I know that isn't true, and I pray that You would renew my hope. I pray that You would work in the hearts of those who do not believe in You. Help me rise above my anger, Lord. Use me to make a difference and to lead others to You.

*"Therefore go and make disciples of all nations, baptizing them in the name of the Father and of the Son and of the Holy Spirit, and teaching them to obey everything I have commanded you. And surely I am with you always, to the very end of the age."*

—MATTHEW 28:19-20

This world can be a difficult place for Christians, and that fact is nothing new. Today's headlines of wars, persecution, and fighting echo the history poured out in the Bible. But when you start to feel angry, frustrated, and hopeless, remember this: God wins! God always wins! Read the words of John 16:33. What are the troubles of this world that you see? Commit to praying about them every day. How might you play a role in overcoming them?

# Pull Me Back to You

Dear Jesus,

I'm slipping away from You. I can feel it, and I don't want it to happen. But it's just been so hard, Lord. You know all that's happened. I'm hurt. I'm disappointed. This isn't the way I thought things would go. And now You seem so far away.

But I love You, Lord. My mind tells me You are faithful, that You are trustworthy. It may not feel that way to me right now—but I *will* believe it. Oh, Lord, help my unbelief.

Open my eyes to Your presence in my life. I know You are here, but I need to see You working in this mess. You promise that if I come closer to You, then You will come closer to me. I'm here on my knees before You. Come to me, Lord, and hold me close. Heal my heart, clear my mind, and strengthen my will.

There's so much I do not know and do not understand. But these things I *do* know: You love me, and I love You. I am Yours. And when I call out to You, You will not let me slip away. I am calling, Lord. Thank You for pulling me back to You.

*"I will search for the lost and bring back the strays. I will bind up the injured and strengthen the weak."*

—EZEKIEL 34:16

When hard times leave you doubting and feeling far from Jesus, it's time to take action. It's time to call out to Jesus. He promised to answer. Read Psalm 145:17–18. How has God shown His faithfulness to you in the past? Can you see glimpses of His faithfulness even in this difficult time? Call out to God, and ask Him to reveal His nearness. Ask Him to pull you back to Him.

# I Tried So Hard

Dear Jesus,

I tried so hard, but I failed. This situation didn't end the way that I had hoped and expected it would, and I am so disappointed. I sought Your will, and I thought I knew what to do. I used great care moving forward toward the goal, and I stopped often to pray. When obstacles got in my way, I asked for Your guidance, and I waited patiently for You to answer me. I was diligent in my work, never giving up. And then, with the finish line in sight, everything came crashing down. I felt as if all my work was for nothing!

Why, Jesus? Why did You allow me to work so hard and get so close just so I would fail?

Oh, but Jesus, as I hear myself pray this prayer, I realize how much of it is focused on me and my efforts. Forgive me, Lord. I don't understand, but I trust You. You will bring good from this, somehow and some way. The rain falls on the just and the unjust. And still I must say—still I choose to say—"Blessed be the name of the Lord!"

*I have fought the good fight, I have finished the race, I have kept the faith.*

—2 TIMOTHY 4:7

Disappointment makes us ask, "Why didn't I . . .? Why didn't God . . .?" Sometimes the Lord allows disappointment in order to build our faith. And sometimes He allows it because He simply has a better plan. But in all things, we must learn to say, "Blessed be the name of the Lord." We must allow God to use our disappointments to strengthen our faith. Think back over the difficult times in your life. Have they drawn you closer to God or taught you to trust Him? How so?

# Trying to Be Perfect

Dear Jesus,

I am so frustrated and disappointed in myself. I want to be better than I am, and I want to do bigger and greater things. I know I'm not being all I can be—not for myself, not for those around me, and definitely not for You.

Lord, I feel as if I have to be perfect all the time. And because I can't be perfect, I feel like a failure. It's putting so much stress on me! I know that only You are perfect and that You don't expect me to be perfect—You only expect me to trust You. But sometimes it's so hard.

In this world, it's all about being on top, being the best. But Your definition of success isn't the same as the world's definition, is it, Lord? Please change my view. Make it match Your own. Show me the life You would have me live—and then please bless me with the courage, strength, and wisdom to live it.

I pray that You would help me be the person You created me to be. Show me the path You want me to follow. I need You, Jesus—and I thank You for hearing me and helping me.

*Let us keep looking to Jesus. He is the one who started this journey of faith. And he is the one who completes the journey of faith.*

—HEBREWS 12:2 NIRV

It is good to want to be just like Jesus, but remember, He is God and the only One who is absolutely perfect. If you feel disappointed in yourself because you expect perfection, it's time to revisit your expectations. It's time to give yourself some grace. God expects you to be faithful, not perfect. Think about the goals, both personal and spiritual, you're trying to accomplish. Are you expecting perfection? In what areas of your life might you need to give yourself some grace?

# Do I Disappoint You?

Dear Jesus,

I feel like such a child—a willful, stubborn, misbehaving child. I've let myself down, and I let You down too, haven't I? Please forgive me, Lord. I'm so very sorry.

I know you understand that I'm a sinner. You don't expect me to be perfect. But I still have to wonder: Are You disappointed in me? I've even avoided coming to You in prayer until now because I've felt so guilty and so ashamed. I didn't want to face You. Instead, I've tried to work up the courage to come to You and be reassured of Your love.

And yet You come to meet me, to comfort me as I pray. I've brought this sin to You, and I can already feel You lifting it away, cleansing my heart and soul. Why do I worry? I know that You love me! Nothing I could ever do would change that. So forgive me, Lord, for my sin and for avoiding You. And thank You for loving me even when I disappoint You.

*Neither death nor life, neither angels nor demons, neither the present nor the future, nor any powers, neither height nor depth, nor anything else in all creation, will be able to separate us from the love of God that is in Christ Jesus our Lord.*

—ROMANS 8:38–39

You never have to run from Jesus when you've done something wrong. First John 1:9 says, "If we confess our sins, he is faithful and just and will forgive us our sins and purify us from all unrighteousness." Is there something you need to confess to Jesus? Pour out your heart to Him here, and let the power of His love and forgiveness heal you.

# Underappreciated

Dear Jesus,

Is it wrong for me to feel underappreciated? I work so hard. I give my time, my effort, and my money. And it's as if no one even notices. Sometimes I have to wonder whether what I do even matters. Would anyone notice if I just . . . stopped?

I know I'm having a bit of a pity party, Lord. And Your Word tells me to serve in secret, to give in secret, but a simple "thank you" would do wonders for my spirit right now. I'm hurt and discouraged. Please clear away these feelings and all the negative thoughts from my mind. Help me see clearly what it is I need to be doing—what You want me to do. Guide me through this dark time with Your perfect light.

You tell me, Lord, that it is more blessed to give than to receive and that in serving others, I am really serving You. So I give myself to You and to Your service. Use my hands, my feet, these gifts You've given me to shine for You. And while I still wouldn't mind a bit of appreciation here on earth, I know that You are smiling down on me from heaven.

*"Do not be dismayed, for I am your God.*
*I will strengthen you and help you;*
*I will uphold you with my righteous right hand."*
-ISAIAH 41:10

Serving others can sometimes be a thankless job, but it's never an unrewarded one. Your heavenly Father sees all the good that you do, and He will reward you (Matthew 6:4). Remember that truth, let it strengthen and encourage you when you feel less than appreciated. Consider all the ways you serve others: Where do you feel unappreciated? Where do you feel you're making a difference? Are there people serving around you who could use a word of thanks?

# Disappointing Others

Dear Jesus,

I hate to disappoint others, but at times I must say no to what they want. You know how many demands are made on my time. If I gave in and accepted every request for my help, I would have no time for You. If I accepted every project—even every good project—I would be neglecting my own needs to have quiet time, to worship, to praise, or simply to rest. Logically, I know this, but I still feel guilty saying no—which too often leads me to say yes when I shouldn't.

It's especially hard with those people who heap guilt on me. I understand how they feel because I'm sometimes disappointed when You say no to me. Yet I understand that when You turn me down, it's for a good reason. Please help others to understand that when I say no, it's also for a good reason. Teach me to bring every request to You, to ask You if I should say yes or no—before I commit to anything.

And dear Jesus, help me realize that it really is okay to say no to others—especially when it means saying yes to You.

*"Cease striving and know that I am God;*
*I will be exalted among the nations,*
*I will be exalted in the earth."*
—PSALM 46:10 NASB

Do you find it hard to say no to others? What would your life be like if you said yes to every request? Would you have time for the things that are most important? Would you have time for God? Make a list of all the things you are asked to do for others. Ask God to sift through your list and help you discern which things need a no and which things need a yes.

# Rejoice in Disappointment?

Dear Jesus,

The apostle Paul said to rejoice in suffering because it gives us strength and builds our character, but that is so much easier to say than it is to do. How can I be happy when disappointment stings so sharply?

Jesus, I confess that I have such a bad attitude right now. I did my best, and I expected to win. I might have been able to muster a smidge of rejoicing and give myself some credit, but only because in the midst of the shock and disappointment of losing I managed to act like a good loser. Why is it so hard to gracefully accept what happened and move on? Why can't I just say, "Oh well" and hope that next time I will do better?

Perhaps I'm being just a little too human today. Remind me, Lord, of all the things I am not disappointed by—things like your infinite mercy and unending love. Remind me that I truly am blessed—even in disappointment. I am blessed because You are my Lord and I am Your child.

*Be of good courage,*
*and he shall strengthen your heart,*
*all ye that hope in the LORD.*
*—PSALM 31:24 KJV*

Disappointment can be a tough thing to swallow. Sometimes all you can do with disappointment is endure it and be grateful—grateful for Christ, for better things to come, for the courage to try again, and for the strength eventually to let go of your disappointment. Has there been a time of disappointment in your life? Will you choose to be grateful for that time? How can you cultivate an "attitude of gratitude," no matter what your circumstances may be?

# Courage to Try Again

Dear Jesus,

I've messed up again. I thought that after so many tries I had finally found the missing piece. I believed that this time I knew how to succeed, how to make it work. But I was wrong.

I feel like just giving up. This road is too long and hard and filled with too many mountains to climb and valleys to struggle out of. I'm tired, and my disappointment wills me to stop trying. Jesus, I'm not sure that I have the strength or the courage to try even once more. Yet there is a voice deep within me saying, "Don't give up. Keep trying. Keep going." Is that Your voice, Lord? Is that what You want me to do?

I have never been a quitter. I have always managed to pull myself up from defeat and try again. But I can't do it on my own. I need You to help me. Perhaps that was the point of this struggle all along—to teach my stubborn heart that I need You, that I can't do it on my own. So will You please give me Your strength? Fill me with Your courage and Your purpose. Guide me in the way I should go—which is ever and always closer to You.

*There is surely a future hope for you,*
*and your hope will not be cut off.*
—PROVERBS 23:18

Martin Luther King Jr. said, "We must accept finite disappointment, but we must never lose infinite hope."[1] Your "infinite hope" is found only in Jesus. Call on Him to help you, to give you the courage and strength to let go of your disappointment and try again. Consider Philippians 4:13, which says, "I can do all things through him who gives me strength" (NIV). What does "all things" mean to you in light of the disappointments you've faced? What does it mean in light of your "infinite hope"?

# You Never Disappoint Me

Dear Jesus,

What would I do without You? You never disappoint me or let me down. Day and night, every day and forever, You are the One who watches over me, protects me, leads me, and loves me. Oh, Jesus, You are so wonderful!

When I am weak, You make me strong. When I am knocked down, You pick me up. Your words soothe and comfort me, and Your example sets me on the right path. When I need to decide, You are the One who makes me wise. You are always with me. You speak to my heart.

Jesus, when the world disappoints me, when life throws obstacles in my way, it doesn't matter because You are my God. Nothing can ever come between us. I know that always You are here, working on my behalf, leading me with Your perfect knowledge toward what is right and good and best.

Dear Jesus, I love You. And I am so thankful for the light of Your presence in my life.

*"I am the LORD;*
*those who hope in me will not be disappointed."*
—ISAIAH 49:23

Because there is sin in the world, there is also disappointment. And sooner or later, disappointment will make its way into your life. But when it does, you can rely on these truths: Jesus will never disappoint you or let you down, and He can even turn disappointments into blessings. Have you witnessed disappointments being transformed into blessings? How does that affect the way you view future disappointments?

# Reflections on Disappointment

# Reflections on Disappointment

# Jesus, I Need Your . . . Faith and Hope

# Light of My Life

Dear Jesus,

Thank You for the gift of light and the joy it brings me.

Sometimes I get up early just to watch the sunrise. I wait expectantly while the eastern sky melts into golden rays. This rising of the sun each morning, Lord—it blesses me with such beautiful proof of your faithfulness, bringing warmth and light to my brand-new day.

Jesus, the truth is that You light up my life all throughout the day—not only with the sun, but also with Your presence. You declared, "I am the light of the world. Whoever follows me will never walk in darkness, but will have the light of life" (John 8:12). All day long Your light warms and guides me; Your love brings joyful brightness to even the darkest days. All around me, I see shining glimpses of You—turning darkness to light.

Then, when evening comes, I watch the sun slip down. Fiery colors streak across the western sky, a blazingly brilliant finale to the day. But even in the darkness of the night, I am not afraid. For You, Lord, watch over me while I sleep.

Thank You, Jesus, for being the Light of my life.

*"I have come into the world as a light, so that no one who believes in me should stay in darkness."*

*—JOHN 12:46*

The third-century theologian Hippolytus said, "A heavenly light more brilliant than all others sheds its radiance everywhere, and He who was begotten before the morning star and all the stars of heaven, Christ . . . shines upon all creatures more brightly than the sun."[1] Jesus *is* the Light of the world. How is He shining in your life? Are you reflecting His light to the world? How can you shine brighter for Him?

# When I Ask

Dear Jesus,

You are amazing. Not only do You give me what I need, but You bless me with so much more than I ask for.

In the book of Matthew, You said, "Which of you, if your son asks for bread, will give him a stone? Or if he asks for a fish, will give him a snake? If you, then, though you are evil, know how to give good gifts to your children, how much more will your Father in heaven give good gifts to those who ask him!" (7:9–11). That means when I ask You for something, You already know whether or not it will be good for me. And if I ask wrongly, You will not give me something that will harm me. You have only good planned for me, and the things You give me will be blessings in my life. But teach me, Lord, to look beyond earthly things for Your blessings; teach me to see the spiritual blessings that come through difficulties and struggles as well.

Jesus, remind me not to limit You by asking only for what I need, but to pray big and with confidence. And always, Lord, help me remember to pray that Your will be done. If I ask in faith and trust in Your goodness, I know that You will bless me with exactly what I need and in ways greater than I ever imagined.

*Now to him who is able to do immeasurably more than all we ask or imagine, according to his power that is at work within us.*

—EPHESIANS 3:20

Could it be that you expect too little from God? Think carefully about what you want, and don't be afraid to pray for something big. Ask God to take your request and refine it according to His will and what He knows is good for you. Then expect Him not only to answer, but also to exceed your expectations. What requests do you have for God? Are they big and bold? Are they for the things of this world or for the eternal things of God?

# Courage to Trust

Dear Jesus,

I want to be more courageous. I *need* to be braver, to be unafraid to step out in faith and follow You. I feel You tugging at my heart, telling me that You want me to do more with the gifts You've given me. But I must confess, Jesus: that makes me nervous and even afraid.

I'm comfortable just the way I am. Change is scary. It forces me to face my fear of the unknown. It's easier when I know exactly what I'm walking into. But You don't work that way. And if I'm to serve You fully, then I can't either.

Teach me, Lord, to step forward in faith, trusting that Your plans for me are good. Jesus, I'm scared. Hold tightly to my hand, and I'll hold tightly to Yours.

Lead me, Lord. And please fill me with the courage to trust You more and to follow wherever You take me. Strengthen me so I can be all that You want me to be. Help me bring glory and joy to You.

*"For I am the LORD your God*
*who takes hold of your right hand*
*and says to you, Do not fear;*
*I will help you."*
—ISAIAH 41:13

It takes courage to move forward into the unknown, and Jesus is the One who can provide that courage. If you hear Him calling you to do something new, trust Him. His plan for you is good, and He will help you fulfill it. Think of the gifts God has given you. Are you using them for His glory? List at least three new ways you can better use the talents He's given you. Pray over these ideas, and then listen for His leading.

# You Are My Hope

Dear Jesus,

You are the source of my hope. When I rise in the morning, you give me the hope of a brand-new day, a clean slate ready to be filled with the best of me. Your hope encourages me to work hard and to be confident that I will meet the day's goals and challenges.

You give me hope all through the day as the demands and pressures of life in this sin-filled world weigh on me. When I ask You to renew my strength and calm my racing mind, You are faithful to do it. You are always present with me, right by my side, helping me and refreshing me so that I might serve You more and accomplish good things in Your name.

And when evening falls, You come to me and whisper hopes of an even better tomorrow. You wash away the mistakes of this day and remember them no more.

Jesus, all the days of my life, my hope lies in You. And even when my days here are done, my hope yet goes on—in the promise of an eternity in heaven with You.

> *Now faith is confidence in what we hope for and*
> *assurance about what we do not see.*
>
> —HEBREWS 11:1

The hope of Christ is not simply some wished-for dream. It's a promise—a promise made by the One who is Himself hope, Jesus Christ. By allowing Jesus to be your hope, you can be confident that He will keep His promises to you. What is your greatest hope? When you know that hope in Christ is not a wish, but rather a promise, how does that affect the way you think about your own hopes for the future?

# The Gift of Hope

Dear Jesus,

Thank You for the gift of hope because it is a gift straight from You. And all You ask for in return is my faith and my obedience.

Before I knew You, life was bleak and uncertain. I often felt lonely and vulnerable. But Jesus, when I found You, all of that changed. As I learned to trust You, hope grew inside me and my future became unbelievably bright.

You strengthen my faith when I read my Bible. You renew my hope with Your sweet words of promise. I put my faith and trust in You.

My hope in You is a gift, given because I truly believe that You are the Son of God and that You love me. You hear my prayers, and I trust that Your answer will always be what is best for me—it will come in Your own perfect way and in Your own perfect time.

*Why, my soul, are you downcast?*
*Why so disturbed within me?*
*Put your hope in God,*
*for I will yet praise him,*
*my Savior and my God.*
*—PSALM 42:11*

Hopelessness is a hollow feeling that can be cured only by a healthy dose of faith in Jesus. When you put your faith in Him, He blesses you with the gift of hope—and that hope is a promise. What are some of your favorite promises from God's Word, the promises that give you hope? How have you seen them kept in your life? In the lives of others?

# Try, Try Again

Dear Jesus,

I feel like a baby learning to walk. I fall down so often, but I try to keep getting back up. I know that I can do anything—anything in Your will—because You are with me. You, Lord, are my hope and my ever-present help.

The enemy is shouting at me to give up, telling me I can't do this. But Your soft whisper drowns out the evil one as You say to me, "Try it one more time."

With sweet, gentle words of reassurance, You lift me up and chase away despair. You encourage me to try new things—even things that some people might think are beyond what I'm able to do. My expectation soars because You and I both know that I can do all things as long as I rely on You and Your strength (Philippians 4:13).

Jesus, some people call me stubborn. Others say that I am determined. But I believe I am simply hopeful—trusting that my Savior will keep the promises He has made.

Jesus, You make all things possible. Thank You for being my hope!

*For with God nothing shall be impossible.*

—LUKE 1:37 KJV

The poet Emily Dickinson described hope this way: "'Hope' is the thing with feathers that perches in the soul and sings the tune without the words and never stops at all."[1] What a lovely way to describe hope in Jesus! What song does hope sing in your heart? Write out the words of your favorite hymn here—or write your own song of hopeful praise.

_____

_____

_____

_____

_____

_____

_____

_____

_____

_____

_____

_____

_____

_____

_____

# Things Unseen

Dear Jesus,

For me, hope comes easiest when life is going my way. But as soon as obstacles block my path, hope turns murky and flounders in the face of a future I cannot see. Even then, Lord, I know that is when I need You most. Restore my hope, my faith in You.

How can I believe in You and *not* hope in the things that are unseen? After all, I've never seen You, yet I believe in You—I *know* You through the truths I read in Your Word and through the reality of Your presence in my heart and in my life. I know that You are here with me. In the past, when I've felt as if my hope was lost, You didn't abandon me. You are faithful to me, Lord, even as I battle to remain faithful to You. And I praise You for that.

Jesus, You are unseen, but You are not unknown—not by me. You are my hope, my promise of wonderful things I can't wait to see!

*But hope that is seen is no hope at all. Who hopes for what they already have? But if we hope for what we do not yet have, we wait for it patiently.*

—ROMANS 8:24-25

Hebrews 11:1 says, "Now faith is confidence in what we hope for and assurance about what we do not see." Faith is the key to hope, and Hebrews 11 is a chapter filled with stories of hopeful people who put their faith into action. Read through Hebrews 11. Which of these "heroes" of faith speaks most to your heart and life? Why?

# Faithful Relationships

Dear Jesus,

I want to be more trusting, and for me, that means making better choices about the people in my life. In the past, I've sometimes chosen poorly and allowed people into my life who have not been guided by You. They've hurt me and let me down. That not only destroyed my faith in people in general, but it also made me lose faith in myself.

Show me how to choose the friends and relationships that are best for me. Bless me with people who not only truly love and care for me, but who also truly love You! That is my prayer, Jesus—that You will help me choose wisely and rebuild my trust in people.

I know that ultimately You are the only One I can perfectly and completely trust because only You are perfect. But there are good people in this world who seek to honor You. Lead me to them—and help me to be one of them.

*Do not be joined to unbelievers. What do right and wrong have in common? Can light and darkness be friends?*

−2 CORINTHIANS 6:14 NIRV

The Bible says that we should not team up with unbelievers (2 Corinthians 6:14). Does that mean there isn't a place for them in your life? No—you are called to be salt and light to this world. But it does mean that you should choose your close friends wisely. Who are your closest friends? Are they faithful to Christ, and do they encourage you to be more faithful? How can you encourage them in their own relationships with Christ?

# Hope for Those I Love

Dear Jesus,

I give my loved ones to You. I give them to You fully, trusting that You will watch over them and care for them every minute of every day. Strengthen them in their love for You.

I know there will still be troubles and trials—these are the inescapable facts of living in this sin-riddled world. But Jesus, please keep my loved ones close to You. Never let them wander from Your side or be tempted into the darkness. Be in their hearts always. Protect them from all harm and evil. Guide the choices they make.

These people, Lord, they are so precious to me. But as much as I love them and as much as I want the best for them, I know You love them even more and Your best for them is better than I could ever imagine. I place my loved ones in Your hands, Lord. Fill them with Your hope.

And I thank You, Jesus, for Your loving and tender care—for me and for those I love.

*The LORD watches over you—*
*the LORD is your shade at your right hand;*
*the sun will not harm you by day,*
*nor the moon by night.*
*—PSALM 121:5-6*

One of the best gifts you can give to Jesus—and to yourself—is entrusting your loved ones to Him. It's not an easy gift to give. But doing so proclaims your faithful trust in Jesus, and it invites Him to lift away your worries and bless you with His peace. Whom will you entrust to Jesus' care? What does knowing that His love for them is even greater than yours do for your worries about them?

# Hope Is Eternal

Dear Jesus,

I must confess that eternity is a concept I don't fully understand. My life is so ruled by time that the thought of an end to time is almost impossible for me to grasp. But the one piece of this puzzle I do understand is that You do not change, not ever, not for eternity.

Everything around me changes—even I change. But You do not, Lord, and that is such a comfort to me. I know that I can depend on You to be the same tomorrow as You are today and as You were yesterday. I can always trust You.

So many people center their hope on earthly leaders, on armies with powerful weapons, on political parties. But the people and things of this world are not eternal; they are always changing. Only You—only Your hope—is eternal.

And so, Lord, I need You. I cling to You—my eternal hope.

*Do any of the worthless idols of the nations bring rain?*
*Do the skies themselves send down showers?*
*No, it is you, LORD our God.*
*Therefore our hope is in you,*
*for you are the one who does all this.*
*—JEREMIAH 14:22*

History holds many valuable lessons for us. And the Bible is, in a sense, a history book. It tells the history of man—of what happens when man puts his faith and hope in God, and what happens when he doesn't. The Bible also teaches us that God's will always prevails, and for those who stand firm in their faith, hope is eternal. Where is your hope centered? Is it in the things, the leaders of this world? Or in the eternal hope of Christ?

# Reflections on Faith and Hope

# Reflections on Faith and Hope

# Jesus, I Need Your . . . Wisdom

# Time-Out, Please

Dear Jesus,

I need a time-out, Lord. I'd like a break from the onslaught of this world's demands. I need a chance to regroup, rethink my strategy, and change my attitude. Or maybe I should say that I need a chance to reconnect with You—so *You* can help me regroup, so *You* can show me Your strategy, and so *You* can reshape my attitude.

This world just keeps coming at me, and so I'm running away. I'm hiding in You, my fortress, my rock, and my shield, just for a little while. Renew me. Give me fresh strength to fight the good fight. Guide me with heavenly wisdom to make the right choices. But for now, Lord, just hold me. Hold me, and let me breathe in Your perfect peace.

There's no peace out there, Lord. But here—with You—all is right, all is calm. Thank You for the time-out, for the time away. You always know just what I need.

*The name of the LORD is a strong tower;*
*the righteous runs into it and is safe.*
*—PROVERBS 18:10 NASB*

This life can come at you at a fast and furious pace. Don't be afraid to step away, to call a time-out and run to Jesus for counsel and care. Consider Psalm 23—it describes the perfect time-out, time away with God. How can you make the time-out with God like the one described in Psalm 23 a reality in your life?

# Dead Ends

Dear Jesus,

I was so sure I was following Your will and taking the path You'd chosen for me. But then I came to a dead end. Jesus, how could I be so wrong? I prayed and asked You to lead me. I meditated on Scripture. In my heart, I thought I knew exactly which way You wanted me to go. But I was wrong. What now?

I'm frustrated, and I guess I'm a little angry too. So I'm taking a deep breath, and I'm reminding myself of who You are and of Your promises to me. If this was a dead end, then it must not have been a good thing for me.

I trust You, Jesus. You have a plan for me; I know it. But I'm a little worried and a little afraid that I'll choose the wrong path again. I wish I had a map that showed exactly where You want me to go and how to get there. I don't know where I'm going, Lord, but I'm trusting You with the next step. You are good and faithful, and You love me. I will follow where You lead.

*Trust in the LORD with all your heart*
*and lean not on your own understanding;*
*in all your ways submit to him,*
*and he will make your paths straight.*
—PROVERBS 3:5-6

Jesus knows exactly where you're going and how to get there, but He doesn't usually show you the destination or the full path ahead. And it's important to remember that even a dead end may be part of His plan. Think of a dead end that you've encountered. Rather than viewing it as failure, ask yourself what you gained from the experience. Did Jesus use it to draw you closer to Him?

# Jesus Understands

Dear Jesus,

Sometimes I behave badly. I don't usually mean to; it just happens. When I feel stressed, overwhelmed, or just plain tired, it's too easy for me to say and do things I later regret. I don't like this part of me. I need Your help to conquer this weakness.

Jesus, You know me so well. You understand my imperfections. You understand when I lose my temper and say things that I shouldn't or when I act out because I'm afraid. When I behave badly—even though I may not understand why myself—You understand me. I'm thankful that You forgive me and provide me with opportunities to try again. When anger or fear tempts me to behave in ways that are not pleasing to You, help me stop and think before I speak or act.

I'm so grateful that You never give up on me. I know You're still working me—and some days, I'm afraid I give You more to work on than others do. Thank You, Jesus, for understanding me—and for loving me anyway.

*For we do not have a high priest who is unable to empathize with our weaknesses, but we have one who has been tempted in every way, just as we are—yet he did not sin.*

—HEBREWS 4:15

When feeling tired or stressed causes you to react in ways that leave you feeling guilty or ashamed, Jesus understands. Bad behavior is part of being human; still, being human is not an excuse for *continuing* to behave badly. Are there things you'd like to change about the way you act? Are there bad habits you've acquired that need to be removed from your life? What good habits can you cultivate instead?

# The Secret of Contentment

Dear Jesus,

I want to be content with where I am in life. But I struggle to find satisfaction in who I am, what I have, and what I've done. Please help me find contentment, Lord.

Your Word tells me that Paul knew the secret of contentment. He said, "I know what it is to be in need, and I know what it is to have plenty. I have learned the secret of being content in any and every situation, whether well fed or hungry, whether living in plenty or in want. I can do all this through him who gives me strength" (Philippians 4:12–13). What is that secret, Lord? Please teach it to me.

I know that the secret begins with trust—trusting You to completely and perfectly meet my needs and relying less on what this world says I need to be happy. So help me trust You, Lord. Teach me to find my contentment in You.

*I have learned to be content whatever the circumstances.*

—PHILIPPIANS 4:11

Contentment doesn't just happen; it comes when you nurture your relationship with Jesus and allow it to flourish. And it begins with complete trust in the Lord. Is there an area of your life that you haven't entrusted to Him? Is it that same area, or another, that is keeping you from feeling content? How might turning it over to Jesus change how you feel about it?

# True Wisdom

Dear Jesus,

You have taught me that true wisdom is found only in You—in studying Your Word, knowing You, and applying Your teachings to my life. The more I read Your Word and talk to You in prayer, the better I know You. And the better I know You, the better I am able to understand what Your Word is telling me and how to apply it. True wisdom does not change with the winds of opinion, as does the wisdom of this world.

Jesus, thank You for teaching me to be wise. I know I have so much still to learn, but by studying the Bible and knowing Your views on what is right and wrong, I don't have to muddle through worldly decisions rife with Satan's tricks.

When I'm not sure about something, remind me that the Bible is my guide. Show me Your promises as I seek Your will. I know that in areas where my wisdom is lacking, You will provide me with Yours.

Thank You, Lord, for the gift of Your wisdom. Your wisdom is perfect truth: it never changes, and it sets me free.

*If any of you lacks wisdom, you should ask God, who gives generously to all without finding fault, and it will be given to you.*

—JAMES 1:5

True wisdom cannot be found in ordinary textbooks. It comes with learning the right way to live in the world—and that knowledge comes only from God and from His Word. The wise person knows what is good and right, acts in that way, and sets a godly example for others to follow. Is there a person of wisdom in your life whom you admire? How has that person been an example to you? How can you be an example to others?

# These Little Ones

Dear Jesus,

This prayer is for the little ones in my world. I want you to open their hearts to receive Your wisdom. Guide them in every choice they make. Help them to make decisions that are good, safe, and right. This world is such a frightening, dangerous place for young people. But You are with them always, Lord. So open up their hearts and pour Your wisdom in.

Jesus, I want them to recognize You and Your voice speaking in their hearts—and not only to recognize You, but also to pay attention to You. When You tell them no, I want them to stop whatever they are doing and follow You instead. When their peers try to get them to do something that they know isn't right, I want them to be brave enough and wise enough to walk away. And when the evil one comes prowling, looking for a soul to devour, be their fortress and their shield. I pray that each and every one of these precious little ones will grow up to love You and to live for You.

Dear Jesus, please watch over these young ones I love.

*The LORD will watch over your coming and going*
*both now and forevermore.*
*—PSALM 121:8*

Whether it's children of your own, nieces or nephews, or children in your church, the young people of today face a complicated and dangerous world. They need the wisdom of Jesus to help them make the best choices. Commit to praying for the children in your life. Write their names here, and then add at least one tangible thing you can do to encourage each child on your list.

_____

_____

_____

_____

_____

_____

_____

_____

_____

_____

_____

_____

_____

_____

_____

_____

# Wisdom in the Storm

Dear Jesus,

The sky has turned dark, and swirling clouds of gray wrap all around me, enveloping me in a dense, foggy mist. I cannot find my way, Jesus. I am lost! I call out to You and listen for Your voice, but I don't hear it. A cold rain pours down on me, and I have nowhere to go. Dear Jesus, tell me what to do. Give me wisdom to endure this storm. I need You!

I *know* You are here, Lord—even if I can't hear You right now. Calm my pounding heart and anxious thoughts so that Your quiet voice can reach me. I run to You, Jesus. Hide me away. Shelter me beneath Your wings.

Dear Jesus, You know exactly what I need. You have the power to end this storm—and I pray that You will. But even if You do not, I will trust You to see me safely through it.

Hold tight to my hand, dear Lord—because I'm holding so tight to You.

Then they cried out to the LORD in their trouble,
and he brought them out of their distress.
He stilled the storm to a whisper.
—PSALM 107:28–29

Have you ever felt so desperate or frightened that you begged Jesus for help? Some storms make us feel desperate—the disciples in the boat knew that (Mark 4:35–41). Some storms come upon us fast, hard, and unexpectedly—they're the kind of storms that only the Lord can rescue us from. Have you ever been hit with unexpected storms? Looking back, can you see the hand of God at work—as He either stilled the storm or walked with you through it?

# To Know You

Dear Jesus,

As always, You have enlightened me through Your Word. In Paul's letter to the Ephesians, he wrote, "I keep asking that the God of our Lord Jesus Christ, the glorious Father, may give you the Spirit of wisdom and revelation, so that you may know him better" (1:17). Jesus, I understand now that when I've asked for wisdom in the past, I was not asking with the right purpose in mind.

Whenever I asked for wisdom, I was often looking only for a solution to a problem. Sometimes You didn't give a clear answer and left the solution up to me. I never understood why. Now I realize that wisdom isn't just about solutions; it's learning more about the One who crafts the solutions. Through every answered request and through every one that is met with silence, I learn more about You.

This then is my request, Lord: in the future, whenever I ask for wisdom, please answer me in a way that will help me know You better.

*Let the one who is wise heed these things*
*and ponder the loving deeds of the LORD.*
—PSALM 107:43

As you read and study God's Word, you'll gain wisdom and insight into His character. When God answers a request for wisdom in an unexpected way or when He remains silent, ask Him, "Lord, what can I learn about You from this?" He will surely give you the wisdom needed to know Him better. Has God ever answered you in an unexpected way? Has He ever answered you with silence? What have you learned about God from His answers?

# Wisdom to Help

Dear Jesus,

I need Your wisdom so I can help another. I've gone through loss in my life, Lord, more times than I like to remember—loss of loved ones, loss of friends, loss of a job. And every time, You've faithfully brought me through that loss. But now, Jesus, I need to help someone else walk through a loss. And just telling her, "Trust in the Lord" doesn't seem to be enough.

Jesus, what can I say and do to help her through this very difficult time? Please fill my mind and my mouth with just the right words, at just the right times—words that bring comfort and encouragement, not additional sorrow or pain. Tell me when to step in and when to step away. And will You please give me a glimpse into her heart, so that I'll know what she needs? And then, Lord, put in my heart the best way to help her. Strengthen me as well so she can lean on me.

Help me to shine the light of Your joy into the darkness of her sorrow. I place my friend in Your hands, Lord. And I thank You for the help and the wisdom I know You will give us both.

*Carry each other's burdens, and in this way*
*you will fulfill the law of Christ.*

—GALATIANS 6:2

Jesus is able to overcome all our hurts all by Himself. But imagine if we all decided that because He is enough, we should just sit back and do nothing. That's not what the Bible says! It holds countless examples of people helping and comforting one another. Think back over the losses you've endured. Who were the people who offered you the greatest comfort? In what ways did they do it? How can you help someone else with what you've learned from them?

# Your Mysterious Ways

Dear Jesus,

So much of what You do is a mystery. I wonder why You choose to be silent sometimes and why You heal some people and not others. How can You be everywhere at the same time and love everyone in spite of their sins? The only answer I have is because You are Jesus—God's own Son, Savior, and Messiah. You are God made flesh and the One whose ways are simply too wonderful for me to understand.

Your mystery intrigues me. Your ways and Your timing are always perfect—though so often I do not understand them. You hear and answer every prayer. You take shattered things and make them whole again. You surprise me, amaze me, and overwhelm me. You are truly awesome, my Lord and my God.

You are a beautifully divine mystery, and though I don't understand You, I put my faith and trust in You. Because there is one thing I know, without a doubt: Your love for me is real, personal, and endless. And for that I thank You, Lord Jesus.

*Surely I spoke of things I did not understand,*
*things too wonderful for me to know.*

—JOB 42:3

It is impossible to completely understand the whys and hows of God, though we often try. We wonder about big things, small things, and all things in between. Sometimes God answers our wonderings, and sometimes He does not. His ways are simply too wonderful, too complicated for us to fully comprehend. What things do you wonder about God? What things do you know about Him? Do the things you *know* affect the way you think about the things you wonder about?

# Reflections on Wisdom

# Reflections on Wisdom

# Notes

## IN PRAYER
1. Corrie ten Boom, *Tramp for the Lord* (New York: Jove, 1978), 140.

## I SURRENDER ALL
2. "I Surrender All," *Hymnary.org*, accessed December 14, 2016, http://www.hymnary.org/text/all_to_jesus_i_surrender.

## THANK YOU FOR JOY
3. Anne Frank, *Anne Frank: The Diary of a Young Girl* (New York: Bantam, 1993), 171.

## THANK YOU FOR LAUGHTER
4. Martin Luther, quoted in *The Westminster Collection of Christian Quotations*, compiled by Martin H. Manser (Louisville, KY: Westminster John Knox, 2001), 225.

## FAITH AND GRACE
5. Charles Spurgeon, "Love: A Sermon (No. 229)," *The Spurgeon Archive*, accessed August 15, 2014, http://www.spurgeon.org/sermons/0229.htm.

## COURAGE TO TRY AGAIN
6. Martin Luther King Jr., *Strength to Love, Fortress Press Gift Edition* (Philadelphia: Fortress Press, 2010), 94.

## LIGHT OF MY LIFE

7. Hippolytus of Rome, *Christian History: Quote of the Week*, posted April 5, 2007, accessed December 14, 2016, http://www .christianitytoday.com/ch/content/quote.html.

## TRY, TRY AGAIN

8. Emily Dickinson, "'Hope' is the thing with feathers," *The Poems of Emily Dickinson*, ed. R. W. Franklin (Cambridge: Harvard University Press, 1999), on Poetryfoundation.org, accessed December 14, 2016, http://www.poetryfoundation.org /poem/171619.